ROOM RECIPES

ROOM RECIPES

A CREATIVE AND STYLISH GUIDE TO INTERIOR DESIGN

TONYA OLSEN

PLAIN SIGHT PUBLISHING

AN IMPRINT OF CEDAR FORT, INC.
SPRINGVILLE, UTAH

© 2013 Tonya Olsen
Photography by Sara Boulter, except pages 50–55 and 216–21
Photographs for Modern Mix Family Room by Jessica Mauss, pages 50–55
Photographs for Natural Selection by Jennifer Hudgins, pages 216–21

ISBN 13: 978-1-4621-1256-2

Library of Congress Cataloging-in-Publication Data on File

Published by Plain Sight Publishing, an imprint of Cedar Fort, Inc.
2373 W. 700 S., Springville, UT 84663
Distributed by Cedar Fort, Inc., www.cedarfort.com

Cover and page design by Angela D. Olsen
Cover design © 2013 by Lyle Mortimer
Edited by Whitney A. Lindsley

Printed in India by Gopsons Papers Ltd

10 9 8 7 6 5 4 3 2 1

{ DEDICATION }

FOR MY MOM AND DAD

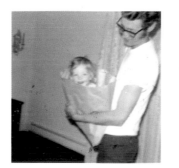

Contents

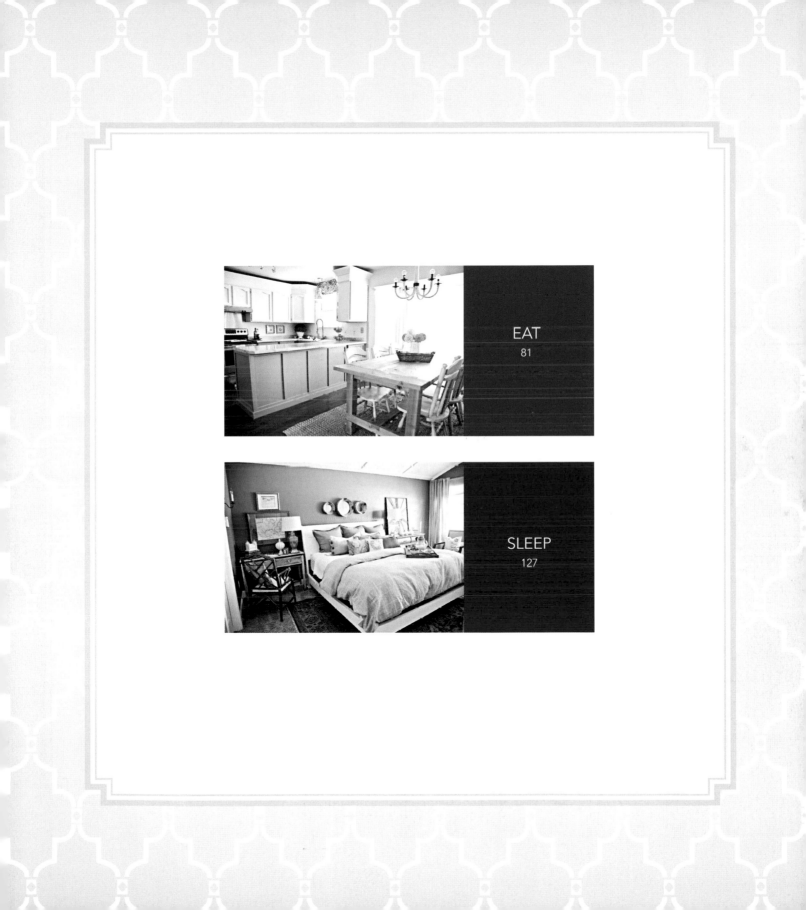

EAT
81

SLEEP
127

"INSPIRATION
IS THE KEY TO
EVERYTHING."

{ OLIVIA WILDE }

Introduction

I've always wanted to create an interior design book full of inspiring interiors and stylish spaces. The idea for this book came one day as I was making dinner for my family from a typical cookbook. It was full of enticing photos with brief yet detailed descriptions, lists of ingredients, and simple instructions for cooking. I suddenly had what Oprah refers to as an "aha! moment." I decided to start gathering a collection of inspiring interior design projects combined with beautiful images and a simple framework to follow and combine them into a cookbook format.

First, let me say this: I can cook, but I am not a chef. I am somewhat lost in the kitchen and have little or no knowledge of exotic ingredients, proper tools, and cooking techniques. I know enough cooking basics to feed my family great-tasting, simple meals that I can easily throw together.

On one hand, I am enticed by the beautiful images of well prepared dishes on Pinterest and tempted by the tantalizing photos on fussy food blogs. I am seduced by the idea of creating a Martha-worthy meal that family and friends will swoon over both in presentation and in taste. On the other hand, I feel completely overwhelmed and intimidated by the process of creating these delectable works of art.

The reality is that I tend to take a casual and spontaneous approach to cooking. I follow recipes to a certain point before adding my own flair. I like to add flavors and spices, substitute ingredients, and use what I have on hand. The end result doesn't always look like the pretty picture, but the meal is uniquely mine—and usually pretty tasty too!

Room Recipes is categorized by type of room rather than by a specific style. In fact, most of the spaces featured in this book are a combination of styles. Each room is personal and unique to the individual who created it. In addition, just as cookbooks often contain different versions of common recipes such as apple pie or chicken noodle soup, *Room Recipes* offers instructions, suggestions, and solutions you may have seen before. The intent is for you to glean ideas and inspiration from the variety of spaces, details, and projects in this book and then add your own spice.

Each room is introduced with a **Palette**, detailing the colors, patterns, and textures in the space. **Ingredients** lists the main components of each room with a brief description of why and how they work. **Room Recipe** provides a generalized set of instructions and ideas for you to consider when designing your own space. Finally, **Garnish** offers simple how-to projects and creative decorating suggestions.

Most important, trust yourself, have fun, and cook up something amazing.

Words of Advice

Words of wisdom from someone who's been there and done that are always beneficial before beginning any project. Whether you conquer projects yourself, hire the necessary professionals or combine a little of both, even a minimal amount of preparation and some sage advice can go a long way in guaranteeing a smooth journey and the ultimate success of your project. The following suggestions are based on my personal and professional experience:

GATHER inspiration and ideas. Online sites like Pinterest and Houzz make collecting and organizing ideas a snap. I'm a bit old school and prefer to create a binder or tote full of samples, images, notes and measurements to carry around as I work on each project. Find the system that works best for you.

DETERMINE the scope of your project taking into consideration time, quality and budget. I adhere to the time-worn adage that you can have it fast, you can have it good, or you can have it cheap . . . pick two! I encourage you to be realistic and honest with yourself. Admit when a task is over your head or consider if a project will take longer than you thought. Manage your spending and hold back when you know you will exceed your budget. Without careful consideration, it's easy to underestimate these important aspects, and projects can quickly spiral out of control.

COMMUNICATE with everyone who will be involved in the decision-making. If you have a spouse, roommate, or other family members to consider, make sure you are aware of everyone's likes, dislikes and overall expectations. If you are working with a professional such as an interior designer or contractor, keep the lines of communication open and honest throughout the process. To every extent possible, make sure everyone is on the same page. Although there may be hiccups along the way, honest communication will save time, alleviate surprises, and prevent unnecessary stress down the road.

CONSIDER existing items. Before I begin any project, I go through a space and take note of what is there. I also encourage clients to make a list of existing furniture and accessories they want to incorporate into their project. Consider new uses for old items. For example, rather than spending money on new lamps, create new ones with a fresh coat of paint. Look at outdated items with an updated perspective.

INVEST in a professional. Notice I used the word *invest* rather than *hire.* Most people minimize the value of involving a professional interior designer or a contractor for bigger jobs. I have many clients who have me fix costly, avoidable mistakes had an interior designer been involved in their project. Although you may ultimately tackle a job yourself, in the very least, an hour or two with a professional can ensure you're on the right track. Even interior designers appreciate feedback and advice from other interior designers!

ACQUIRE a set of basic tools and supplies. I recommend having these items on hand no matter how little or how much you plan to do yourself. These are the items I use the most:

Hammer

Phillips Screwdriver

Flathead Screwdriver

Tape Measure

Level

Staple Gun

Glue Gun

Sandpaper

Painter's Tape

Duct Tape

Picture Hanging Kit

KNOW that there will be stressful moments and frustrating circumstances. You may experience thoughts of self-doubt, moments of utter chaos, and episodes of sheer panic. Do not worry. This is normal. Take a deep breath and count to ten. There is light at the end of the tunnel, and it will be worth it in the end.

EXPECT the unexpected. Subs will not show up, furniture will be backordered, and that bathroom remodel will have unforeseen issues that no one would have anticipated. Obviously, the larger and more complex the project, the greater odds that something may go awry. When problems occur, the challenge faced is not the mistakes, but your attitude toward them. Keep things in perspective and, as they say, don't sweat the small stuff.

BE flexible and take risks. When a space doesn't feel right, move things around or rearrange if necessary. Get rid of items that don't work. Be willing to deviate from your original plan or vision. For example, that peacock-blue loveseat you had in mind might not be the best fit for the space after all, or consider what it might look like to paint the ceiling black. Being open to all the possibilities will release limitations and allow creativity to flow.

FILL in the gaps. During every project and especially toward the end, I continually assess missing décor. Keep an eye out for that perfect painting or antique chair that you know would make the space complete. It's tempting to buy something, even though it's not quite right, just to finish a project or fill a space. Be patient. That perfect item will come along.

TAKE your time. Interior design shows make it appear that entire homes can be perfectly decorated practically over night. If you've recently moved into a home, live in the space for a while before purchasing furniture and accessories. If you want to remodel your kitchen, take time to plan for exactly what you want. A truly creative and stylish space evolves over time.

ENJOY the process. A relaxed approach to interior design is the key to making every project successful.

WELCOME

1

First Impressions

If the **eyes** are the **windows to the soul**,

then the **entryway** is the **window to the**

home. This **happy home** welcomes every

guest with **color**, **personality**, and **charm**.

PALETTE

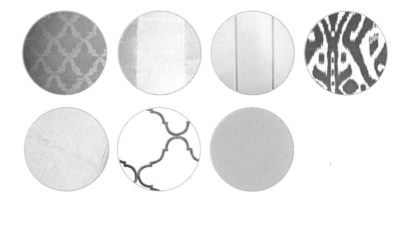

BEFORE

{ INGREDIENTS }

1 ## DESK AND BOOKCASES
A traditional farmhouse table, converted to a desk, fits snugly between two bookcases. The shelves showcase various collections while the open backs reveal the pretty wall pattern.

2 ## CONSOLE TABLE
A repurposed cabinet hutch makes an excellent console table.

3 ## STORAGE BENCH
Fabric paint goes a long way to give the outdated upholstery on this storage bench new life.

4 ## SEATING
Classically designed Lucite chairs provide additional seating. The transparency doesn't compete with the colorful flavor of the room.

5 ## WALL TREATMENT
The eye-catching wall pattern reflects major sparkle. Glitter was added to a tinted glaze before being stenciled on the walls.

6 ## LIGHTING
Glamorous light fixtures throw dramatic patterns across the walls and ceiling while leading guests into the main area of the home.

7 ## FLOORING
This area rug was painted slightly imperfect to create a handcrafted look in this high-traffic area. The distressed finish easily hides dirt and can be cleaned with mild soap and a damp rag.

ACCESSORIES
An abstract collection of accessories line the open bookcase shelves. A punch of emerald green mixes things up a bit and adds unexpected, welcome touch.

ROOM RECIPE

{ TONYA'S TAKE }

I literally jumped up and down when I entered this house. It's so full of energy! While the entry itself is small, consisting of the area directly in front of the door including the console, the open floor plan makes the home feel larger than life. Guests are immediately drawn in to the creative soul of the home.

COMBINE cottage charm with glamorous flair. Add pizzazz such as glitter, crystal, and gold paint to secondhand, repurposed items.

ARRANGE furnishings along the perimeter of the room to create an open space plan. This arrangement encourages guests to sit around the edge of the room, leaving the center of the room open.

SUBSTITUTE expensive store-bought items with creative DIY alternatives. Nearly every item in this entryway was restored and reinvented.

DISPLAY family photos in colorful frames and personal mementos on open shelving. Guests will immediately feel a sense of connection to the space.

SPRINKLE with simple, decorative do-it-yourself projects to add a personal sense of accomplishment.

{ GARNISH }

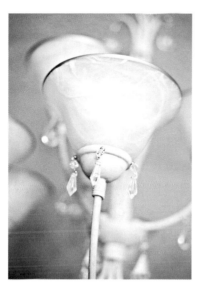

Refurbished Chandelier

Take an outdated light fixture and a little paint to create a stunning chandelier. Magnetic glass crystals add a touch of sparkle.

Ingredients:

Metal or iron light fixture with glass shades

Spray paint in the color desired for the fixture

Metallic craft paint for detailing

Magnetic glass crystals (available at craft stores)

Small craft paintbrush

1. Remove glass shades and bulbs from light fixture.

2. In an open, well-ventilated area, evenly spray paint on fixture in light, consistent strokes until color is even. Let dry.

3. Using the metallic paint and small paintbrush, carefully paint a thin line around the rim of the shade. Repeat as necessary until paint is even. Let dry.

4. Replace glass shades.

5. Install light fixture.

6. Place crystals evenly around the base of each shade and throughout the fixture.

> **TONYA TIP:** Consider adding magnetic crystals to common flush mount dome fixtures, a standard feature in most homes.

A Welcome Home

Symmetry is a key design element in the **Colonial-style home**. The interior rooms are designed around the centrally located **entrance, hallway,** and **staircase**. What a **perfect way** to make a **grand entrance!**

PALETTE

BEFORE

{ INGREDIENTS }

1 LIGHTING
A low-profile light fixture is perfect for a room with low ceilings. The quatrefoil shape dresses up the space.

2 SEATING
A vintage settee welcomes guests and provides a spot for guests to kick their shoes off.

3 FLOORING
An indoor/outdoor rug in a dark color protects the wood floors, hides dirt, and is easy to clean. The graphic trellis motif adds a burst of visual interest.

4 TABLE
A small, simple side table provides a place to drop keys and loose change.

5 STAIRWAY
A gallery wall of family portraits, prints from vacations, and cherished art introduces guests to the family.

6 COAT HOOKS
Birds take shape as coat hooks and add a touch of playfulness. The hooks are installed low enough for children to easily reach.

7 PILLOWS
Chevron, burlap, and birds are a fun mix of pattern, texture, and theme.

ROOM RECIPE

{ TONYA'S TAKE }

The "informal formalness" of this Colonial-style entry is what makes this entryway unique. The entryway feels stately while projecting playful character.

MAKE the entryway serve its purpose. An indoor/outdoor rug for wiping feet, hooks for hanging coats and bags, and an antique settee for waiting guests creates a multifunctional, welcoming space.

DISPLAY collections of artwork starting with a focal point at the landing of the stairs. Hang a combination of artwork in mismatched frames diagonally up the wall leading the eye to the top of the stairs.

MIX and match a variety of geometrical shapes and patterns including chevron, clover, and trellis.

KEEP original architectural elements such as the formal wainscoting, dark-stained oak floors, and traditional stair balusters. Update with furniture, accessories, and décor.

{ GARNISH }

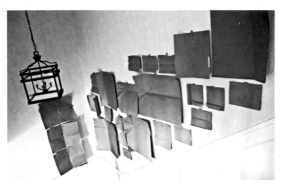

Stairway Art Gallery

Hanging an art gallery wall isn't as tricky as it sounds. The best way to avoid what is referred to as the "shotgun" approach (randomly hammering an array of nails into the wall), is to create paper templates you can easily arrange on the wall prior to final installation.

Ingredients:

A variety of artwork in mismatched frames, assorted sizes, and different mediums

Paper large enough to trace the shapes of the frames onto

Pencil, scissors, hammer, painter's tape, level, nails

1. **Trace** each piece of artwork onto a piece paper; mark an X on the location where the nail will go.

2. **Cut** shapes out of paper carefully.

3. **Place** a small piece of painter's tape onto each piece of paper.

4. **Arrange** the paper templates visually, following the angle of the stairs. Start by anchoring the bottom of the gallery with the largest piece of paper.

5. **Tape** templates onto wall. Try various layouts. Don't worry about making mistakes.

6. **Once** arrangement is final, hammer a nail through the X into the wall.

7. **Remove** templates one at a time and replace with original artwork.

8. **Use** a level to ensure that everything is hanging straight.

> **TONYA TIP:** If you're more adventurous and aren't afraid of making holes in your wall, skip the templates and spontaneously hang the artwork. Unorganized, casual arrangements look best loosely arranged.

HOMEOWNER &
DESIGNER:
Sara Boulter

Photo Finish

Creative features including **chalkboard**
and **Instagram walls** impart many
delightful comings and **goings**.

PALETTE

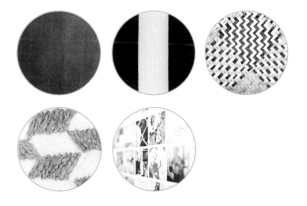

{ INGREDIENTS }

1   BENCH
Kick off your shoes and stay awhile! A seated bench next to an entry door is a practical necessity. Rustic iron legs and a wooden seat are simple and solid.

2   RUG
Bold contrasting stripes make a big statement by making this small entryway feel wider.

3   CHALKBOARD WALL
A chalkboard wall adds a creative architectural element to the space. A fine coat of chalkboard dust mutes the intensity of black wall.

4   WALL TREATMENT
An impactful and unexpected floor-to-ceiling collage of Instagram photos literally brings life to this space.

5   WALL HOOKS
Tree branch wall hooks provide a clever spot to hang bags, coats and more.

ACCESSORIES
A vintage mail organizer is the perfect spot to drop the mail; framed artwork in subtle tones brings balance the bold elements of the room; a starburst mirror made of driftwood repeats the tree branch element; and pillows in muted tones add texture and interest while softening the space.

ROOM RECIPE

{ TONYA'S TAKE }

Technically the mudroom, I'd be tempted to skip the front door and bring my guests through the garage just so they could experience this playful space.

COVER an entire wall with an unexpected element to create an eye-catching and interesting focal point. Instagram pictures add personality while showcasing the family's adventures.

SIMPLIFY accessories within a small yet dynamic space. Accessorize with a palette of soft, neutral colors to prevent visual competition with stronger elements

AVOID letting the mudroom become a dump zone. As obvious as it sounds, store shoes under the bench and hang coats on hooks. If necessary, add baskets, shelving or bins to keep things organized and to manage clutter.

BALANCE large patterns with small prints. The chunky contrasting stripes of the rug coordinate with the small Instagram images.

USE a reversible flat-weave rug in a mudroom. The thin weave allows the door to swing into the room without getting caught up. Reversible rugs can be turned over, extending the life of the rug. Flat weave rugs are also easy to clean.

{ GARNISH }

Instagram Wall

Pull those Instagram photos off your device and plunk them into your décor!

Ingredients:

Instagram photos

Image editing software

Printer

8.5″ x 11″ paper

Repositionable spray adhesive

1. **Import** Instagram photos into an image-editing or collage generating program.

2. **Determine** the shape and size for each image.

3. **Crop** and scale images to predetermined size.

4. **Place** images in a linear grid format, filling the 8.5″ x 11″ paper space.

5. **Print** images and trim edges as necessary.

6. **Spray** the back of each sheet with adhesive and stick to the wall, lining each sheet next to each other until the entire wall is covered.

Light House

Nestled in the foothills of Utah,

the **open** and **expansive** entry of this

classic Hampton-style home offers

a **majestic view** of the valley below.

PALETTE

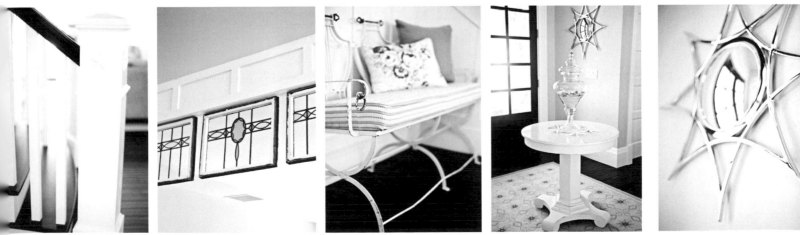

{ INGREDIENTS }

1 STAIRCASE

This grand staircase has classic architectural details and clean lines. The white balusters offset the dark wood stain of the floor and handrail.

2 ANTIQUE WINDOWS

Stained-glass windowpanes add a whimsical touch attached to the ceiling of the adjacent dining room.

3 LIGHTING

A classic chandelier with shades provides light without distracting from the rest of the home.

4 ENTRY TABLE

A round pale-blue table takes center stage in the entryway.

5 HARDWARE

Vintage glass hardware is an unobtrusive yet formal touch. The faceted surface reflects light.

6 RUG

A vibrant area rug in beachy hues anchors the entry table and ties together the colors in the adjoining rooms.

ACCESSORIES

Starfish surround an apothecary jar full of seashells and introduce the coastal style of the home.

ROOM RECIPE

While this home is quite majestic, the simple furnishings in the entryway—a small table, a jar full of seashells, and an antique bench—don't compete with the architectural details and the view.

SIMPLIFY furniture and accessories in a grand entrance so the focus stays on the view of the valley below.

REPEAT shapes. The round shapes in the rug duplicate the round table and round chandelier. The round shapes offset the linear balusters on the staircase.

KEEP architectural colors neutral when the walls of open adjoining rooms have vibrant colors.

HIDE storage under the stairs with a secret door. This clever design feature keeps clutter tucked away and the focus on the architectural details.

ACCESSORIZE a casual bench with a comfortable seat cushion and colorful pillows. The small touch of color introduces the vibrant colors in the adjacent rooms.

{ GARNISH }

Creative Suggestion

The space under the stairs conceals a hidden closet within the board and batten finish work. It provides storage without announcing its presence.

WHEN THE homeowners moved to Utah from a coastal town, they wanted to bring the beach with them. This house perfectly reflects their love of a light, bright, breezy style.

TONYA TIP: Trade throw pillows out seasonally but within the same color scheme to keep the entryway fresh.

LIVE

29

HOMEOWNER:
Brooke Karras

DESIGNER:
Deboni Sacre

Assisted by
Samantha Zenger &
Sarah Wolfley

Color Down Under

Far from feeling like a dingy, dark basement, this **light** and **airy family room** comes alive with **vibrant pops of color.**

PALETTE

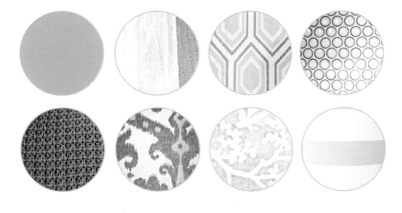

{ INGREDIENTS }

1 CONSOLE

A simple console with clean lines was built by hand and painted white. Orange metal stools make it both fun and functional.

2 CHAIR

This darling accent chair was a great find at HomeGoods. The electric ikat design coordinates perfectly with the room.

3 MEDIA CABINET

A local craftsman built this custom media cabinet to fit perfectly in the space.

4 OTTOMAN

A tufted, iridescent denim ottoman is uniquely detailed with chartreuse nail heads and piping to create a dynamic feature in the room.

5 WINDOW TREATMENTS

Faux roman shades are layered over a bamboo roller shade. A subtle hint of chartreuse binding accentuates the edges and ties into the other colors in the room. A stagecoach valance on the French door in contrasting colors is both functional and fun.

6 WINDOW SEATS

Cushioned window seats with a variety of throw pillows create a cozy spot for cuddling up with a good book.

7 FIREPLACE

Rather than using a common material such as stone or porcelain tile on the fireplace surround, a soothing glass mosaic adds beauty and interest.

8 LIGHTING

This room contains a variety of lamps in different colors and patterns. Using the same bold colors found in other accessories create unity and bring everything in the room together.

ACCESSORIES

A subtle version of the bright coral in the room, stained-glass bottles capture the light in the kitchenette, flanked with a colorful apothecary jar full of yummy candy; smoky, textured glass vases symmetrically line the center of the console table; embroidery hoops in various sizes display playful swatches of fabric to create a simple wall arrangement; throw pillows in a kaleidoscope of colors and patterns adorn the sectional; and weathered gray cabinet knobs add character to the media cabinet.

ROOM RECIPE

This delightful family room contains a variety of patterns and splashes of vibrant colors. The room feels bright and playful, perfect for entertaining friends and family.

ADD visual interest with finish work like the wall treatment behind the television. The V-groove panels are painted a light steel blue.

INCLUDE traditional furniture and décor that coordinate with the style in the rest of the house. Adding a few modern touches like the fire-orange barstools makes the space unique.

SPRINKLE a repeated color theme throughout the room. Variations of coral, chartreuse, sky blue, and teal draw the eye around the room and make it feel cohesive.

PLACE plenty of seating options for a variety of activities around the room. Barstools under the console are a perfect spot to enjoy refreshments. A large sectional with a chaise and upholstered ottoman are a great addition to put your feet up on and watch TV.

Embroidery Hoop Wall Display

This inexpensive and fun project adds color, shape, and pattern in a delightful wall display.

Ingredients:

An assortment of embroidery hoops in various sizes

An assortment of fabric swatches in various colors and patterns

Scissors

Craft glue

1. Cut fabric slightly larger than each hoop size.

2. Unscrew the fastener on hoop and place the inner hoop underneath the fabric.

3. Smooth fabric and replace outer hoop on top of inner fabric.

4. Adjust fabric until pattern is centered and fabric is taut. Retighten fastener.

5. Trim excess fabric leaving about ¼" around.

6. Apply a thin line of glue to inner edge of hoop and firmly press fabric into place until bond forms.

7. Repeat steps 1–6 for each hoop.

8. Arrange and hang hoops in a creative wall display.

> TONYA TIP: Rather than displaying the hanging embroidery hoops on a wall, create a decorative mobile using fishing line to hang from the ceiling.

Project by Samantha Zenger

HOMEOWNER:
Kathleen Hermann

DESIGNER:
Rick Boyles

Gypsy Gem

An extra bedroom filled with salvaged furnishings was converted into an **intimate family room** for **lounging, visiting,** and **watching TV.**

PALETTE

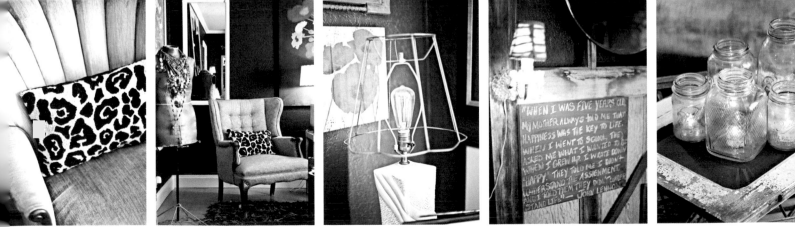

{ INGREDIENTS }

1 CHAIRS
Vintage chairs, found at a local flea market, have been repurposed as casual seating.

2 MEDIA CABINET
The doors were removed from the closet, and a console table serves as a media cabinet.

3 COFFEE TABLE
An old chicken coop makes a fascinating and unique coffee table.

4 WINDOW TREATMENTS
Simple window treatments soften the room and block light while watching movies.

5 WALL TREATMENT
The ceiling was painted sky blue to match the floor and brighten the small space. Crown molding separates the ceiling from the dark walls.

6 ART
One of the few original (and expensive!) objects in the room is an oil painting by the homeowner's favorite artist, Sherry Dooley.

7 FLOORING
A former basketball gym floor was rescued after a tornado damaged a local school. A large, gently used leather rug anchors the room.

ACCESSORIES
A well-worn mannequin displays an assortment of jewelry; a glass jar of paintbrushes make a creative accessory while reflecting the homeowners artistic flair; a creative fix for an old lamp shade provides ambient lighting; and mason jars serve as candle holders.

ROOM RECIPE

This room is cozy, intimate, moody, and stimulating all at the same time. These items, collected over time, have become some of the homeowner's favorite possessions. I like that the room is small enough for groups of people to engage in intimate conversation.

REMOVE the fabric from old, dated lampshades to expose the wire frame beneath and to create an unexpected piece of art.

ORIENT the furniture to encourage conversation. In small rooms, it serves to arrange furniture against the walls, leaving the center of the room open.

CONVERT odd, rarely used space into something functional. An extra bedroom, formerly used for storage, makes a quaint family room.

REMOVE doors from a closet to create a media nook. The recessed space accommodates the large television, leaving more space in the room for seating and guests.

CONSIDER the unlimited possibilities of salvaging secondhand furniture and found objects into decorative and useful items. After all, one man's trash is another man's treasure.

{ GARNISH }

Barn Door Display

Transform an old door into a piece of art. A decorative door with unique characteristics or elaborate detailing can serve as a piece of art within itself. The large flat surface of a door makes a great space to hang decorative items such as mirrors, artwork, wreaths, and frames. If the door is too large or too heavy to hang, simply lean it against the wall.

TONYA TIP: Old doors are often weathered and warped. Be sure to remove broken glass, lead paint, or any sharp objects such as nails or hinges.

WHILE CLEANING out my grandparents' storage shed a few years ago, I rescued two interior doors from my great-grandparents' first home in America. My great-grandparents immigrated to Minnesota from the former Yugoslavia in the early 1900s. With meager financial means and abundant natural resources, they built everything by hand, including the doors. On display in my home, the doors are treasured family heirlooms that I will cherish forever.

Suitcase Storage

In a small room with limited space, use old suitcases, hatboxes, and trunks for storage. Suitcases are functional yet decorative, and their contents are easily accessible.

TONYA TIP: Look for luggage from different eras to fit the style of your decor. Each generation had its own design and unique features.

HOMEOWNER &
DESIGNER:
Rachel Jones

Assisted by
Tonya Olsen

Barn Dance Family Room

A renovated basement family room

offers the **perfect hangout spot**

for **friends** and **family.**

PALETTE

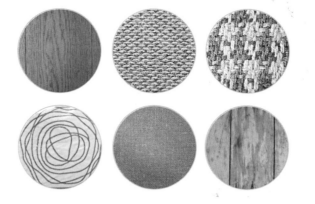

BEFORE

{ INGREDIENTS }

1 SECTIONAL

A massive sectional provides ultimate seating space for family and friends. It can be configured in a variety of ways.

2 CHAIRS

Vibrant teal chairs provide additional seating while adding color to a previously neglected corner.

3 BARN DOORS

Built by hand, the custom designed barn doors add rustic charm and privacy when needed.

4 ISLAND

A small island in the kitchenette gives guests a place to sit while enjoying refreshments.

5 PUB TABLE

A pub table serves as an area for playing games. The weathered finish and metal legs give it a casual feel.

6 ARTWORK

Personal photos from a recent trip to Paris frame the corner of the room.

7 FLOORING

A natural area rug in an exaggerated houndstooth pattern covers the floor beneath the sectional. The rug adds texture and variety to the room.

ACCESSORIES

Pops of orange, teal, and green enliven the space and make it come to life. The accessories are arranged to lead the eye throughout the room.

ROOM RECIPE

{ TONYA'S TAKE }

A few coats of fresh paint transformed this space from a rarely used, rustic basement to an updated, lively family room. The homeowners reluctantly removed a hand-scraped log chair rail that they had cut down, finished, and installed themselves. Way to go!

USE existing architectural details. The exterior of the cabinets, island, and tongue-and-groove paneling were simply altered with paint.

DIVIDE space into separate functional areas. The long length of this room allows it be divided into several multipurpose spaces.

MIX and match an assortment of throw pillows in various sizes, shapes, colors, and textures. The pillows break up the large scale of the sectional while providing visual appeal.

INVOLVE the entire family in your renovation. Give everyone a paintbrush and let them go! Many hands make light work.

ACCESSORIZE a family room with retro movie theater props. A vintage stage light and antique movie reel add fun flavor to the space.

Sliding Barn Doors

Interior barn doors are all the rage. They add rustic charm and create an illusion of space beyond the door opening. Unfortunately, custom barn doors and hardware can be expensive! If you are on a budget and aren't afraid to tackle a weekend do-it-yourself project, this is the job for you.

These sliding doors were modified and customized using Ana White's barn door project guide. Project information can be found at ana-white.com.

TONYA TIP: Use reclaimed wood for a completely rustic look. Nicks, dings, and knots add character.

HOMEOWNER:
Tricia Swesey

DESIGNER:
Tonya Olsen

photography by
Jessica Mauss

Modern Mix Family Room

This **family room** provides **ample seating** for social gatherings, creative storage solutions, and **bursts** of color, texture, and character.

PALETTE

BEFORE

{ INGREDIENTS }

1. SECTIONAL
A large, brown leather sectional provides ample seating and durability. The clean lines and neutral color make it a great transitional piece to coordinate with many styles.

2. CHAIRS
Gray, modern wingback chairs provide additional seating.

3. MEDIA CABINET
A glass-door media cabinet is decorative yet functional.

4. COFFEE TABLE
An industrial coffee table with metal frame and casters add a rustic touch.

5. WINDOW TREATMENTS
Linen window panels mounted close to the ceiling visually add height. Layered over plantation shutters, they add softness to the room.

6. WALL TREATMENT
Horizontal, distressed wood paneling adds character to the nook and sets the stage to display the TV.

7. ADDITIONAL STORAGE
Repurposed nightstands provide additional magazine storage, while labeled baskets neatly contain the kids' games, books, puzzles, and toys.

8. FLOORING
Layered rugs add texture and dimension. A large natural area rug defines the sitting area, while a smaller wool rug on top anchors it to the room.

ACCESSORIES
A yellow serving tray holds odds and ends, television remotes, and a canister of snacks; glossy orange table lamps add not only light, but a punch of color to the corners of the room; a mixed media wall collage creatively displays the homeowner's personality; and colorful pillows in geometric patterns tie it all together.

ROOM RECIPE

I love this room for the variety it offers. When I was growing up, our home had a formal living room, a casual family room, and a basement recreation room. Each room was separate and had its intended purpose. This multipurpose space offers it all. Plus, it has plenty of room for a multitude of family and friends.

COMBINE modern and traditional styles. The clean lines of the sectional complement the exaggerated design elements of the traditional wingback chairs.

ARRANGE furniture to create a comfortable and open area for socializing. The wingback chairs balance the sectional to create a functional, symmetrical layout.

ADD personal items, colorful accessories, and functional storage. Each item in the gallery wall has significant meaning to individual members of the family. Pillows and lamps add vivid contrast to the neutral foundation of the room. Baskets, drawers, trays, and canisters are placed in various locations throughout the room.

MIX textures to create variety and interest. The soft wool rug offsets the rough consistency of the natural area rug beneath it. The smooth leather on the sectional contrasts the textured upholstery on the wingback chairs. Reflective, mirrored media cabinet doors offset the rustic wood paneling.

SPRINKLE with simple, decorative do-it-yourself projects to add a personal sense of accomplishment.

DO NOT FIGHT WITH CHRISTOPHER!
DO NOT

WASH
SHARE EVERYTHING

PORT ST. LOUIS

RHÔNE

FRANCE

LIFE IS
BEAUTY
FULL

{ GARNISH }

Reverse Plywood Silhouettes

This is a fun alternative to the standard silhouette artwork. The grain of the plywood adds interest to the profile image of your choice. Don't be limited by size or subject matter!

Ingredients:

Sanded plywood cut to size

Profile of choice

Acrylic paint in color of choice

Small can or spray of clear wood varnish

Pencil, scissors, square-edge paintbrush

1. Cut plywood to desired size if necessary.

2. Print or draw silhouette of choice on a piece of paper

3. Cut out the silhouette carefully, being sure to include details such as eyelashes.

4. Position the silhouette on the plywood and trace lightly around it with a pencil.

5. Use the flat edge of a paintbrush to carefully paint around the outer edge of the silhouette.

6. Holding the paintbrush at a 45-degree angle, continue to fill in the negative space around the profile using smooth, consistent brush strokes. Paint to the edge and along the sides of the plywood until it filled in.

7. Let dry completely.

8. Apply a single coat of varnish with a clean brush, and let dry.

9. Apply an additional coat of varnish if necessary. Let dry.

TONYA TIP: Consider an interesting subject matter such as common objects with distinct lines and interesting shapes.

RECENTLY, while cleaning out a closet, Tricia discovered an actual set of house rules that her older sister had created when they were kids. Rather than display the original copy, Tonya imported the rules into a graphic design program and creatively rearranged them into a work of art.

House Rules

For a fun family activity, gather everyone together to create a personal set of house rules. Using typefaces in various sizes and fonts truly make this a work of art.

Ingredients:

10–20 personalized house rules

Word processing or graphic design software

Printer

Frame and mat (optional)

1. Type rules into word processing or graphic design program.

2. Use the editing feature to arrange rules creatively in various fonts, colors, and sizes.

3. Print, frame, and display!

TONYA TIP: Focus on uplifting, positive "do" statements rather than discouraging "don't" statements. Have a sense of humor.

Coastal Casita

The **multipurpose space** contains areas

for **sleeping, lounging,** and **cooking.**

This **contemporary guesthouse** provides

plenty of space for **out-of-town guests.**

PALETTE

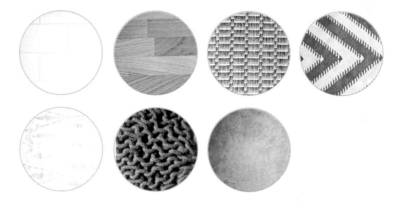

{ INGREDIENTS }

1 LOVESEAT

Because space is limited, a small loveseat was incorporated into the furniture arrangements. The classic, nail-head trimmed design contrasts with the modern elements of the space.

2 CHAIR

Wicker chairs bring the outdoors in. The texture offsets the clean, white walls.

3 COFFEE TABLE

An organic wood base topped with a sleek sheet of glass keeps the room from feeling cluttered.

4 PILLOWS

Throw pillows in complementary hues add interest and depth. A furry pillow adds a whimsical touch.

5 GALLERY WALL

The uniform symmetry of the gallery wall creates a creative focal point while adding a personal touch.

6 BED

A comfy bed sits beneath a vintage window mirror. The wicker bench at the end of the bed balances with the wicker chairs in the living area.

7 KITCHENETTE

A small kitchenette is a must have in a guesthouse. Clean, contemporary cabinets provide ample storage for flexible storage needs. Floating shelves display a collection coastal accessories.

ACCESSORIES

Organic, fun, and fresh, the minimalist accessories in this space make a statement without overwhelming the space.

ROOM RECIPE

{ TONYA'S TAKE }

A casita is a small, relaxed place for guests to stay, separate from the main house. The coastal décor makes this an inviting and versatile space to comfortably receive guests year round.

KEEP a clean foundation, such as white walls and concrete floors, and add furniture and décor in bright colors sparingly.

COMBINE multifunctional areas for eating, sleeping, and lounging, into one large room for guests to enjoy all the comforts of home.

COLLECT souvenirs from family trips and favorite destinations. Share them with guests by using as accessories and décor.

STAIN a concrete foundation instead of installing traditional flooring. Concrete floors are easy to maintain and durable. Area rugs add warmth, softness, color, and texture.

ADD plants to create a living oasis of décor. Plants can be strategically placed to fill dead corners, hide outlets, and add a bit of life to any space.

{ GARNISH }

Custom Coffee Table

Sometimes finding the right coffee table seems impossible, especially if a non-standard size, color or shape is required. Creating the perfect table for your space is easy following these simple instructions.

Ingredients:

- Two stools or base options of your choice approximately 16″ in height
- One sheet of tempered glass at least 12 mm thick with beveled edges, cut to size
- Rubber dots

1. **Position** the base in front of your seating area.

2. **Place** one rubber dot in each corner of base.

3. **Carefully** place glass on top of base.

> **TONYA TIP:** Consider using actual wood stumps from a tree that has meaning to you and your family. Ceramic garden stools are another fun option to add color and interest.

Windowpane Mirror

Create the illusion of a framed window by adding mirrors by following these simple instructions.

Ingredients:

- Wooden windowpane
- Mirror pieces, cut to size
- 150-grit sandpaper
- Primer
- Paint color of choice
- Window and door silicone

1. **Sand** windowpane in long even strokes. Wipe dust with damp cloth.

2. **Prime** the front and back of the windowpane. Let dry.

3. **Paint** windowpane in even coats until consistently covered. Let dry.

4. **Lay** mirrors face down from the back of the windowpane.

5. **Apply** window and door silicone to the back edge of each mirror to secure in place. Let dry.

> **TONYA TIP:** Explore local antique shops and flea markets for vintage windowpanes. If the windowpane is warped and weathered, skip the paint and let the rustic character shine through.

HOMEOWNERS:
Anthony and
Bershunda Taylor

DESIGNER:
Kara Paslay

Fuchsia Fantastic Living Room

This **family room** is the **main living space** for **hanging out with family and friends, watching TV, and gathering around the fireplace**. The **vaulted ceilings, stone fireplace surround**, and **rustic beams** contrast with the **unique décor,** creating a **rustic modern vibe.**

PALETTE

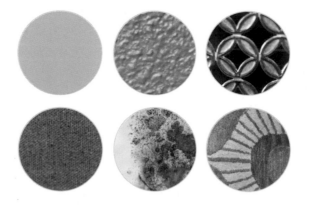

{ INGREDIENTS }

1 ## OTTOMANS
Two identical ottomans sit side-by-side to create a version large enough for the scale of the room.

2 ## CHAIRS
Rolling office chairs, a low-cost flea market find, were effortlessly stained with fabric dye and sprayed with a generous coating of fabric protector to keep the color in place.

3 ## CABINET
Another flea market treasure, this antique cabinet was updated with a few coats of chalk paint. The gold-leafed decorative molding makes a swank statement.

4 ## SIDE TABLE
Textured wood baths cover a cylinder filled with a lightweight concrete substrate to make an ingenious, decorative side table.

5 ## LIGHTING
A table lamp with a clear glass base keeps the focus on the artwork behind it.

6 ## WINDOW TREATMENTS
Dark lilac curtain panels add a touch of glamour for a fraction of the cost of custom panels. These panels come in extra-long lengths so they can easily be tailored to fit your space.

7 ## FLOORING
An oversize wool rug grounds the room. The exotic pattern, which fully exposed might feel overwhelming, peeks out beneath the furniture.

ACCESSORIES
Plants are must-have accessories. They add life, color, and shape to nearly every room in the house. Additional accessories cast subtle hints of the family's love for the beach: mini buoys, a sea salt crystal, and dip-dye art.

ROOM RECIPE

{ TONYA'S TAKE }

Rustic architectural elements contrast with vibrant accents (did you notice the neon hurricane artwork?) to create an eclectic balance. The secret to making a room like this work is to follow basic design principles like balance, rhythm, scale, and proportion. Definitely one of my favorites!

SEARCH for gently used furniture, like the rolling office chairs and cabinet, at secondhand shops, flea markets, and online classifieds. A little TLC can bring them back to life and up to date.

INSTALL window treatments in a room with a vaulted ceiling at same height as the top of the adjacent walls. This visually lowers the ceiling, making the space feel more intimate.

ADD subtle references of personality. The hurricane artwork may seem random, but the homeowners attended college where the team mascot was a hurricane.

PAINT the bottom one-third of a room with high ceilings a dark, rich hue to keep the eye grounded and to balance the dark, rustic beams.

{ GARNISH }

Dyed Chairs

Give outdated upholstery new life with fabric dye. Easily create a custom color for the perfect match.

Ingredients:

Large plastic container

Fabric dye

Paintbrush

Spray on fabric protector

1. Mix dye solution in large plastic container by following package instructions. Stir well to make sure color is evenly dispersed.

2. Apply dye to fabric with paintbrush, using smooth, even strokes.

3. Let fabric dry.

4. Spray a liberal amount of protector on fabric in slow, even strokes.

> TONYA TIP: Embellish the trim of your newly dyed chair with decorative nail heads.

Juju Wreath

A Juju is an African ceremonial tribal hat made of fluffy feathers. In this instance, it reminds the homeowners of their heritage and makes for a vibrant focal point over the fireplace.

Ingredients:

Large plastic container

Cardboard

Styrofoam wreath form

Flat black spray paint

Black gaff tape or black duck tape

White or colored feathers

Dye (optional if using white feathers)

Hot glue gun

1. Mix dye solution in large plastic container by following package instructions. Stir well to make sure color is evenly dispersed.

2. Immerse feathers in dye solution for several minutes.

3. Take feathers out once they are your desired shade and let them dry. Fluff dry feathers if necessary.

4. Trace Styrofoam wreath form on cardboard and carefully cut out the shape.

5. Spray paint the circle cutout with flat black paint.

6. Wrap black gaff tape or duct tape around the outside of your wreath form.

7. Place the spray painted cardboard circle on top of the Styrofoam wreath form and secure with gaff tape or duct tape.

8. Dab hot glue, starting on the outer edge, on stem of feather and apply to wreath. Continue around the wreath, moving toward the middle until wreath is full.

9. Use the void created by the wreath form to hang your handmade Juju on the wall.

> TONYA TIP: Create a Juju using colored feathers that have symbolic, specific meaning. For example, red feathers represent vitality and confidence; magenta feathers represent prosperity; and blue feathers represent truth and spirituality.

Colonial Overture

A collection of antiques, do-it-yourself projects, and custom furniture creates a symphony of beauty in this renovated Colonial home.

PALETTE

BEFORE

{ INGREDIENTS }

1 SOFA
A white slipcover covers a standard sofa frame and adds a feeling of tranquility to the space. The slipcover can be thrown in the wash for easy cleaning.

2 CHAIRS
Classic club chairs finish off the seating arrangement. The small scale keeps the space open.

3 CABINET
An antique hutch was updated with a creamy coat of chalk paint. The scale and size of the piece anchors the space and provides storage for displaying collectible items.

4 OTTOMAN
A large, casual upholstered ottoman grounds the space. A serving tray on top provides a flat surface for food, drink, and other items.

5 WINDOW TREATMENTS
Inexpensive curtain panels were detailed with vertical banding to add interest and to create visual height. The neutral color and linen fabric add softness to the space.

6 WALL TREATMENT
A creative display of sheet music flanks the hutch and serves as a wall treatment. A whimsical pattern was printed on each sheet and mounted a swath of linen. Each song has personal meaning to different members of the family.

7 GAME STORAGE
A repurposed bookshelf doubles as a sofa table and a spot for storing games. Tucked behind the sofa, it's easily accessible to the adjacent game table.

8 FIREPLACE
Seating is conveniently placed around the focal point of the room, the fireplace. A colorful painting above the mantel brightens the space and commands attention.

ACCESSORIES
Classic glass and silver candlesticks line the mantel, asymmetrically framing the bold artwork; a bowl of pinecones makes a simple accessory; a serving tray rests atop the upholstered ottoman; throw pillows layer the seating throughout the room; and a stack of antique books adds height, interest, and color to a side table.

ROOM RECIPE

{ TONYA'S TAKE }

This creative homeowner was not afraid to invest in an interior designer to help her with space planning, color coordination, and installation. Involving a professional is well worth the investment.

CHOOSE a slipcovered sofa for versatility and easy cleaning. The creamy slipcover on the sofa can easily be thrown in the wash when necessary. The neutral color goes with any décor.

HANG a vibrant work of art above the fireplace to create a focal point. Glass and silver candlesticks flank at different heights, creating visual interest and asymmetrical balance.

MIX multiple shades of one color to create a formal yet playful vibe. Blue is the soothing color of choice in this living room, varying from bright cobalt blue in the artwork to soft sky blue on the walls and every shade in between.

PAINT furniture a solid color using hues from the statement piece above the fireplace. The large antique hutch contrasts the touch of white in the painting; the bookcase behind the sofa is red like the boat; and the end table between the club chairs is a rich navy found in the waves on the water.

ADD crown molding around the top of the walls and the ceiling. This simple ornament draws the eye up, distinguishes the color of the walls from the color of the ceiling, and stays true to the formal Colonial style.

{ GARNISH }

Sheet Music Art

Compose a harmonious series of framed sheet music. Let each member of the family choose a favorite song or meaningful lyrics that will sing in your space.

Ingredients:

Computer and printer

Several sheets of music

Digital vector artwork of choice

Spray glue

Linen fabric

Frames

1. Search the Internet for free vector artwork in ornamental or floral patterns. Select a different graphic for each sheet of music.

2. Import vector image into software program and adjust to a coordinating color.

3. Print vector artwork onto a blank piece of paper, making sure image is correctly positioned to print on top of sheet music.

4. Place sheet music in printer tray and print.

5. Apply a light coat of spray glue to the back of each finished sheet of music.

6. Adhere to linen fabric and center in frame.

7. Repeat steps 1–6 for each image and corresponding sheet of music.

8. Hang in a creative arrangement on the wall.

TONYA TIP: For an eclectic look, use different sizes, vintage sheets of music combined with new ones, and various shades of paper.

Sweater Pillow

Recycle an old sweater by turning it into a comfy pillow cover.

Ingredients:

Sweater

Pillow insert sized to fit within cover

Buttons

Measuring tape, needle, thread, scissors

TONYA TIP: If you don't have an old sweater in your closet to spare, you can find a plethora of chunky, textured, and patterned sweaters at your local thrift store. Be sure to wash or dry clean before you make your pillow.

1. Cut two sweater panels, one from the front and one from the back of sweater, 1" larger than pillow insert.

2. Thread the needle and knot the end.

3. Align sweater panels back to back and sew three sides together. Turn cover inside out.

4. Place pillow insert inside of cover.

5. Measure equally and use a pen to mark on the open edge, where you want the buttons to go.

6. Position buttons and sew on one at a time.

HOMEOWNER:
Lauretta Sechrest

DESIGNER:
Deboni Sacre

Assisted by
Jenna Rix

Color Theory

A **navy** and **white color palette** accentuated with **silver** and a **punch of teal** creates a modern and vivacious family room.

PALETTE

BEFORE

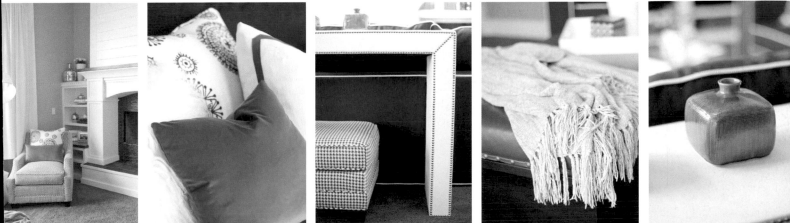

{ INGREDIENTS }

1 SECTIONAL

A navy herringbone textile contrasts the stark white welt on the oversize sectional.

2 SEATING

A classic club chair dressed in navy and cream houndstooth provides additional seating.

3 CONSOLE

Edgy meets elegant in custom designed upholstered console. Textured faux leather trimmed with chrome nail heads combine to make sophisticated and stylish piece.

4 WINDOW TREATMENTS

Banded, two-tone drapery panels frame the massive windows. The dark contrasting color on the bottom pulls the eye down from the dramatically high ceiling.

5 FIREPLACE

Classic millwork and V-groove paneling create a dramatic focal point on the fireplace. Open shelving displays accessories and allow easy access to equipment. Linear glass tile adds contrast on the surround.

6 OTTOMAN

An oversize storage ottoman stores extra blankets and pillows. The neutral brown leather and warm wood coordinate with many styles.

ACCESSORIES

Mercury glass containers filled with fresh flowers peek from the top shelf of a built-in bookcase; shiny chrome and glossy ceramic accessories accentuate the fireplace; a white-and-silver tray holds a small succulent and keepsake box; and an odd-numbered grouping of throw pillows in a variety of textures and colors feels fresh and sophisticated.

ROOM RECIPE

{ TONYA'S TAKE }

A monochromatic color scheme is a great way to add drama and contrast to your space. Navy, the dominant color in this family room, looks striking next to white accents and details.

PAINT millwork and cabinetry white for a classic, timeless look.

TOSS metallic accents into a monochromatic color scheme. As a general rule, use cool metals such as nickel, chrome, and steel with cool colors and warm metals such as copper, bronze, and brass with warm colors. The polished chrome nail heads and mercury glass accessories infuse this relaxed family room with a glamorous touch.

GROUP items similar in color and finish, such as a set of chrome vases, for a cohesive impact.

THROW a soft blanket across a large ottoman to soften a space.

SPLASH a single complementary color throughout a room with a monochromatic color scheme. Hints of teal in the accessories and throw pillows add dimension and interest throughout the room.

{ GARNISH }

Creative Suggestions

Turn an unused corner into a built-in desk or bookcase. The dead space behind the sectional was easily transformed into a functional nook. A suspended slab of wood was installed at counter height below built-in open shelving. Because the space is tucked away, it can even feel somewhat private no matter how many people are in the room!

EAT

81

DISHING UP SOME DIY
108

PLACE SETTING
114

WHITE DONE RIGHT
120

HOMEOWNERS:
Garth and
Natalie Renfrow

DESIGNER:
Kara Paslay

Industrial Farmhouse Dining Room

Originally, this home addition was a stuffy formal dining room. With **industrial**, **farmhouse**, and **vintage accents**, it's been transformed into a casual, family-friendly gathering place.

PALETTE

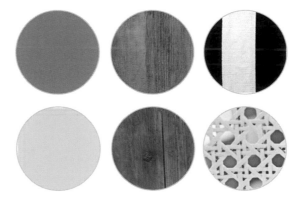

{ INGREDIENTS }

1 DINING TABLE

A salvaged trestle farmhouse table provides seating for up to ten guests.

2 DINING CHAIRS

Industrial metal chairs offset the vintage farmhouse table. The height of the upholstered linen captain chairs is proportionate to the size of the table. A colorful scarf adds a pop of color.

3 BUFFET CHEST

A vintage family dresser was repurposed as a buffet chest. Bright blue paint feels chic against the original hardware.

4 SEATED BENCH

A seated bench was built to create a nook between two built-in storage closets. The doors of the closets were removed and the background painted bright yellow to create fresh, open shelving. Wood planks were installed horizontally behind the bench. The planks were washed with a homemade gray stain to create an aged, weathered look.

5 LIGHTING

Inexpensive metal barn lights were painted John Deere green to create a farmhouse classic. The unsightly cords are intertwined with heavy rope, adding interest and charm. A flea market find, rustic tractor axles were converted to table lamps.

6 ADDITIONAL STORAGE

Vintage suitcases and trunks provide storage for items that are used less often.

7 FLOORING

Two 8″ x 10″ broad striped rugs overlay each other to create one oversize rug large enough to hold the table and chairs.

ACCESSORIES

"WE" is spelled out in large-scale metal letters to represent the importance of family. It is the perfect accessory to fill the empty space above the bookshelf and along the vaulted ceiling. Children's artwork and family mementos support the casual feel of the dining room. Living plants as a centerpiece provide color, texture, and shape.

ROOM RECIPE

{ TONYA'S TAKE }

What a refreshing alternative to the formal dining room. The spectacular interior of this room is perfectly designed to take advantage of the natural light. Massive windows bring the outside in and create a conservatory feel to the space.

CONSIDER how your family lives when designing a room. Do you have a large family? Do you entertain a lot? Is your style casual or formal?

TOSS some throw pillows and a blanket into a built-in nook, even in the dining room. Snuggle up with a good book while taking in the beauti ful view.

CHOOSE dining room furniture to accommodate the maximum number of guests. Consider an extension or drop leaf table to add length, which can often double the amount of seats.

REMOVE doors from closets to create open display shelves. Paint the backs of the shelves a vibrant color to draw the eye in.

BRING balance to a room through repetition. The industrial metal dining chairs are echoed in the rustic metal lights. Warm gold tones repeat from one end of the room to the other in the mirror above the buffet, the wood of the table, and the yellow walls behind the shelves.

Weather Gray Wood Stain

A nontoxic, eco-friendly alternative to store-bought wood stain, this do-it-yourself version can be customized to a specific color and intensity. Keep in mind that the type of wood you use will also affect the color. For a gray finish, oak is a good choice.

Ingredients:

- Stainless steel scrubber or steel wool
- Glass jar with lid
- Distilled white vinegar
- Paintbrush

1. **Place** steel in jar and add vinegar. Be sure to make enough stain for your project. Cover with lid.

2. **Soak** the wool for at least 24 hours. The longer it soaks, the darker the stain.

3. **Test** the stain by applying it to a piece of scrap wood.

4. **Apply** stain to final project with paintbrush. The stain will go on clear and continue to darken.

5. **Let** the stain dry and apply another coat if necessary to create desired result.

TONYA TIP: Replacing the steel wool with different types of metal changes the color. A handful of pennies will create a patina color while the iron in some rusty nails will produce a dark charcoal color.

Savvy Scarf Style

I'll stick my neck out on this one and suggest that using a scarf as a home décor accessory is brilliant!

Creative Suggestion:

Liven up a neutral upholstered chair by draping a folded scarf over the back of it. Since the types of scarves sold in stores vary seasonally, switch out colors and materials depending on the time of year.

TONYA TIP: Not only can you swap scarves seasonally, you can also switch them out for entertaining. Coordinate scarves with holidays throughout the year or to coordinate with a party theme, such as a baby shower.

I OFTEN shop with the intention of creating something amazing out of something ordinary. I look for average items and figure out how to liven them up, add my personal touch, or use them in a different way. Use coat hooks, for example, to hang pots and pans in the kitchen.

Design Outside the Box

Think beyond the typical use of an object to create something completely original.

Creative Suggestion:

Use vintage metal file boxes as centerpiece planters

Turn a tractor axle into desk lamp

Use a sheet of moss as a table runner

Gold Leaf Luxury

What's for dinner?

Undaunted elegance.

PALETTE

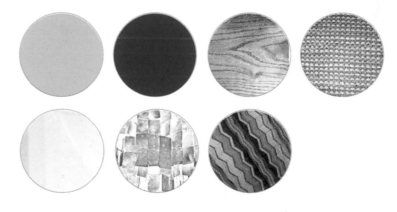

BEFORE

{ INGREDIENTS }

1 TABLE

A distressed walnut table provides seating for 6. Its warm wood finish and classic tailoring is basic enough to go with any style.

2 CHAIRS

Ghost chairs add a hint of visual interest without competing with other features of the room. Linen armchairs are jazzed up with a colorful scarf.

3 ARTWORK

Neon pops of color in the artwork make a bold statement without overpowering the space.

4 LIGHT

Shimmering gold layers of semitransparent Capiz shells create an organic yet elegant look. The light fixture's oversize scale makes a big statement. Track lighting in the nook adds dimension by bouncing off the wall tiles.

5 WALL TREATMENT

Dimensional wall tiles add an abstract element of texture, depth, and visual interest. Random tiles were painted gold to break up the white.

6 FLOORING

A natural woven sisal rug adds a touch of texture yet transitions seamlessly onto the hardwood floor.

ACCESSORIES

The dramatic style of this room begs for simple accessories to make the room complete.

ROOM RECIPE

{ TONYA'S TAKE }

Despite the glamorous appeal of this dining room, if you look closely, it has simple elements with a few amazing details. In fact, the homeowner's original walnut table even works in the space when surrounded by sparkle and sass.

CREATE a dramatic, dimensional feature wall in a room with minimal or simple decor.

LINE a rectangular dining table with a full-length runner. The runner anchors the multiple vases used as a centerpiece.

PAINT the bottom half of a wall a vibrant color to jazz up any space. The bold color below the chair rail coordinates with the pops of color throughout the room.

INCLUDE a large potted plant. The vertical, organic element adds height and dimension while reflecting shadows of light. Fiddle-leaf fig trees are fairly easy to maintain, which makes them an excellent choice.

{ GARNISH }

Gold Leaf

Gold leafing or "gilding" is the ancient technique of embellishing surfaces with an antiqued veneer of hammered gold. It is an inexpensive and easy way to add a little bling to just about anything!

Gold leafing is a great way to add elegance to a space. Simple leafing is sold at most craft stores in adhesive sheets and paint. Use gold leaf to highlight details and create dimension. Simply follow the package instructions for the method you prefer.

> **TONYA TIP:** Gilding isn't limited to gold. Silver, copper, and other metals provide an equally rich metallic luster.

Photoshop Artwork

If you want to create a look that is more unique than just hanging up some printed-out pictures, use Photoshop to enhance or change the colors. A simple adjustment can turn a regular photo into a work of art!

Charmed, I'm Sure

Classic **wallpaper** adds **formal flair** to this dining room, while **antiques** and **hand-me-down furniture** keep the space **casual**.

PALETTE

{ INGREDIENTS }

1 HIGH CHAIR
A vintage high chair, passed down through generations, was painted a rich red, adding an unexpected pop of color to the room.

2 CHAIRS
Antique Chippendale chairs were updated with a fresh, neutral coat of paint to contrast with the velvety hue on the lower half of the walls.

3 WALL TREATMENT
Pairs of quaint lovebirds nestle among creamy ferns and spots of golden pigment in this classic wall covering. The chair rail and lower half of the wall are painted a dramatically rich hue.

4 TABLE
An old, neglected table comes to life and finds a new purpose with a fresh coat of off-white paint.

5 WINDOW TREATMENTS
Smocked window panels frame a floor-to-ceiling wall of plantation shutters. The sheer fabric softly diffuses the natural light while adding softness to the space.

6 PLATE ARRANGEMENT
To avoid competing with the ornately patterned wallpaper, a collection of simple white plates and platters were arranged on the wall in an eye-pleasing composition.

7 LIGHT
A striking, oversize wrought-iron lantern serves as a focal point over the dining table.

ACCESSORIES
Strategically placed pops of color add flavor to the space without overwhelming the room.

ROOM RECIPE

{ TONYA'S TAKE }

Dinner is served without the stuffy formal feel that most traditional dining rooms have. Although the style of chairs is formal, the seats are covered in a textured vinyl, so spills and messes from the kids are easy to wipe up.

PAINT the bottom portion of a wall a rich, dark color in a room with low ceilings. The dark color anchors the space, while the white ceiling keeps the room feeling spacious and open. The dark band of crown molding ties everything together.

AVOID hammering nails into expensive wallpaper by using adhesive hooks that can easily be removed without damage when necessary.

CONVERT an old dresser into a serving buffet. The drawers have plenty of space to store silverware and linens.

COLLECT an assortment of secondhand white dishes. Mismatched patterns make for whimsical place settings or interesting décor.

LEAN a mirror against the wall to reflect light and visually enlarge the space.

{ GARNISH }

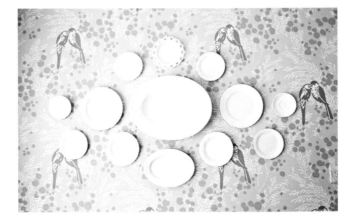

Hanging Plate Collection

Symmetrically hanging a plate collection requires a bit of planning and preparation. This type of arrangements works well in a more formal setting.

Ingredients:

Adhesive plate hangers

Collection of dinnerware

Measuring tape

Painter's tape

Craft paper

Nails or adhesive wall hooks

1. Secure adhesive plate hangers to dinnerware.

2. Measure the area on the wall where arrangement will be displayed, noting the height and the width.

3. Use painter's tape to measure off the same dimensions of the wall on a nearby area on the floor.

4. Trace each piece of dinnerware onto craft paper and carefully cut them out to use as a pattern.

5. Experiment with a variety of layouts using the dinnerware patterns in the taped-off area on the floor, until a satisfactory arrangement is determined.

6. Use the layout on the floor as a guide and place a small piece of tape on each dinnerware pattern and duplicate layout on wall.

7. Hammer nail or install adhesive wall hook under each pattern once layout is evenly spaced on wall. Keep in mind the location of each plate hanger since they will vary in location from item to item.

8. Remove patterns from wall and hang dinnerware, gently pressing each item flush against the wall.

> TONYA TIP: For an eclectic look, collect an assortment of dishes in various patterns, styles, shapes, and sizes. If you prefer a more uniform look, gather pieces in a matching color from a single pattern.

Capturing the Season

Winter, the **seasonal results** of a **personal color analysis**, comes alive in a **glamorous dining room**. Rich, vibrant colors such as **black**, **white**, and **indigo** contrast with **light**, **icy finishes** such as **chrome** and **glass**.

PALETTE

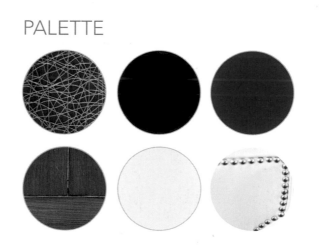

BEFORE

{ INGREDIENTS }

1 DINING TABLE

The massive weathered patina farm table anchors the space while providing seating for multiple guests. The warmth in the wood tones down the rich colors.

2 SEATING

The scale of these modern wingback chairs balances the generous table and traditional dining chairs. Stark white leather and polished chrome nail heads turn this classic chair into a magnificent transitional piece.

3 LIGHT

Chrome and crystal finishes are luxurious accents to a winter color palette.

4 WINDOW TREATMENTS

The stark black pleated shades add another level of glamour. Crisp white linen, another winter characteristic, contrasts with the rich, blue walls.

5 CEILING

The sharp angles of the white, coffered ceiling are accentuated by a simple molding.

6 BUFFET

A functional console serves as a dining buffet. The open shelves provide plenty of storage for large platters and other dinnerware.

ACCESSORIES

A glass and chrome lantern is flanked on each side by a cylinder hurricane creating a simple centerpiece while echoing the Winter theme; a gallery wall features iconic destinations of the homeowner's personal travels; and a pop of red, another Winter color, accents a fresh bouquet of white daisies.

ROOM RECIPE

{ TONYA'S TAKE }

Infusing the palette of your personal color analysis into your interior creates harmony and balance beyond your wardrobe. Combined with standard interior design principles such as scale, balance, and harmony, this dining room gleams with sophisticated charisma.

IDENTIFY your personal color palette and incorporate it into your interior design. Personal color palettes are typically divided into seasons: Winter, Spring, Summer, and Fall.

COMBINE sleek, shiny surfaces with natural, organic elements to create textural difference. Contrast can apply to texture as well as color.

CONTRAST dark walls with white accessories and trim. The light color keeps the room from feeling closed in. Dark and light are classic Winter characteristics.

REPEAT elements. This basic interior design principle creates balance. The shape of the black shades on the chandelier is repeated in the table lamp on the buffet.

SPRINKLE with sparkle. Shiny chrome, clear crystal, reflective mirrors, and gleaming glass add a finishing touch to the Winter palette.

{ GARNISH }

Creative Suggestions

A professional color consultation can reveal the best colors not only for your wardrobe but also for your home. Often categorized by season, here are the most basic characteristics of each:

1. WINTER: Dark, cool, bright, royal blue, emerald green, black, white

2. SPRING: Light, warm, bright, salmon, periwinkle, warm gray, ivory

3. SUMMER: Light, cool, muted, pale pink, violet, medium blue, off-white

4. FALL. Dark, warm, muted, chocolate brown, olive green, burgundy, off-white

HOMEOWNER &
DESIGNER:
Pamela Jensen

Dishing Up
Some DIY

With a **limited budget**, a little bit of **elbow grease**, and **few coats of fresh paint**, this homeowner transformed a dated kitchen from plain old shabby to **shabby chic.**

PALETTE

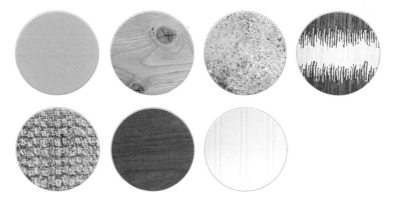

BEFORE

{ INGREDIENTS }

1 CROWN MOLDINGS

Builder's grade oak cabinets, popular 20 years ago, were instantly updated with wide crown molding in a simple profile.

2 CHAIRS

Rustic dining chairs were painted powder blue and then distressed, adding charm to the casual farmhouse dining table.

3 CABINETS

Painting the kitchen cabinets resulted in the biggest bang for the buck. A few coats of Nuvo cabinet paint resulted in upper cabinets contrasting the velvety gray base cabinets. Titanium Infusion was used on the upper cabinets to contrast the Slate Modern base cabinets.

4 TABLE

A rustic farmhouse table was built by hand and crafted to the perfect size for the space. Extensions allow the table to expand for additional seating.

5 WINDOW TREATMENTS

Simple curtain panels are layered over off-white roller shades, providing privacy while still allowing light to softly permeate the room.

6 COUNTERTOPS

Giani countertop paint transforms outdated laminate countertops. The stone texture adds a high-end, look without the expense of real granite.

7 CHANDELIER

An inexpensive store-bought light fixture was easily transformed with some twine and globe-shaped light bulbs, adding a touch of rustic charm above the table.

8 RUGS

A natural woven jute area rug grounds the dining table and chairs. The chunky weave adds texture and dimension without overwhelming the small space. A graphic cotton rug, which is easy to clean, adds a bit of oomph in front of the sink.

ACCESSORIES

Clear glass canisters visibly display baking ingredients; a set of hand-drawn prints adds interest to the white backsplash; a potted topiary adds life to a shadowy corner; and blue and white ticking stripes provide pattern and privacy in the window above the sink.

ROOM RECIPE

{ TONYA'S TAKE }

The light, airy colors and antiquated furniture in this renovated kitchen remind me of a sunny summer day. The most remarkable aspect about this kitchen makeover is that the big changes didn't require a big budget.

COMBINE soothing shades of blue-gray, creamy white, and apple green to create a welcoming kitchen color palette.

ADD architectural interest by installing strips of MDF board to replicate the look of board and batten on the island.

HANG vinyl textured wallpaper in place of a traditional backsplash. Textured wallpaper comes in a variety of embossed textures and patterns. Leave it white or paint it a color to complement your space.

INSTALL modern track lighting to illuminate a narrow space. A white finish discreetly blends in with the ceiling.

SPLASH a touch of glamour throughout by installing crystal cabinet hardware. This affordable option dresses up the cabinets and makes a dazzling impact.

{ GARNISH }

Farmhouse Table

Home improvement blogger Ana White features do-it-yourself instructions for building a custom farmhouse table in her book, The Handbuilt Home. These instructions were modified from Ana's detailed plan, which can be found at ana-white.com.

Ingredients:

4   8'-long 2 x 4s

1   10'-long 4 x 4

4   6'-long 2 x 8s

1   8'-long 2 x 8

1   6'-long 2 x 10

3" screws

2½" pocket screws

Wood glue

Wood stain

Polyurethane

Paintbrush

Finishing supplies

Tools:

Measuring tape

Chisel

Square

Level

Pocket hole jig

Circular saw

Drill with counter sink bit

1. Cut wood to length.

2. Cut notches in legs and stretcher support using circular saw and chisel.

3. Attach stretcher support to legs.

4. Drill pocket holes in small apron and attach to legs using 2½" screws.

5. Attach long aprons to legs using pocket holes and 2½" screws.

6. Attach stretcher with 3" screws.

7. Build tabletop using pocket holes and 2½" screws.

8. Attach breadboard ends to tabletop with pocket holes and 2½" screws.

9. Lay tabletop face down on flat surface and attach apron and legs using pocket holes and 2½" screws.

10. Sand table until smooth. Remove residue by wiping with a damp cloth.

11. Finish using colored wood stain of choice. For best results, use wood conditioner before staining.

12. Apply polyurethane topcoat for protection.

Jute-Wrapped Light Fixture

This is a simple way to add natural texture to a common chandelier by wrapping it in twine.

Ingredients:

Chandelier light fixture, preferably with classic lines

Jute twine

Black spray paint, optional

Globe-shaped lightbulbs

Hot glue gun

Tape

1. Securely tape twine at the inner edge of a single arm.

2. Wrap twine around fixture to cover tape.

3. Continue to wrap twine tightly and evenly around arm, occasionally placing a small dab of hot glue to hold twine in place.

4. Secure twine at the end of each arm with a dab of hot glue.

5. Repeat steps 1–4 around each arm of fixture.

6. Repeat steps 1–4 around base of fixture.

7. Install light, insert bulbs, and enjoy!

Place Setting

This **timeless kitchen setting** combines

traditional features with **modern**

conveniences and **creative flair**.

PALETTE

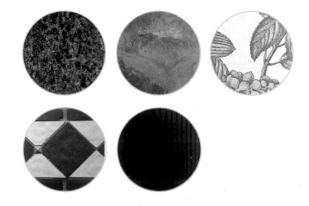

BEFORE

{ INGREDIENTS }

1 HARDWARE

Hand-painted ceramic knobs add charming detail to the island. Each knob has its own unique pattern and design.

2 BARSTOOLS

The sleek lines on these modern barstools complement the classic features in this kitchen. Finding the proper scale in proportion to the island is an important consideration when selecting the right barstools.

3 HANGING POT RACK

A metal pot rack creates a functional focal point for displaying pots, pans, and utensils. Hanging it over the island keeps everything within reach.

4 REFRIGERATOR STORAGE

Reminiscent of a vintage pantry, miniature chalkboards clearly label the contents within the wicker baskets in the refrigerator.

5 FLOORING

Custom made 12 x 12 concrete tiles adorn the floor in a checkerboard pattern. Notice the bronze accent tiles adorning the perimeter.

6 LAMPS

Crystal-based table lamps provide ambient lighting and add understated elegance to the island. Holes drilled in the soapstone countertop discreetly guide each electrical cord to an under-counter outlet.

ACCESSORIES

A petite cake pedestal holds an assortment of spices; a decorative light switch cover adds detail to an otherwise conventional component; a relic light box illuminates a variety of mini cereal box covers; a collection of white dishes are neatly stacked upon stainless steel shelves; and a custom-built ledge displays vintage family recipes in mismatched frames.

ROOM RECIPE

{ TONYA'S TAKE }

Architect and interior designer Robert McArthur has a timeless, eclectic style. A vital component of Robert's design is his attention to detail. He intuitively knows how to combine classic features with modern elements to create a style that is uniquely his own.

SEASON every detail with creative flair. With a bit of imagination, everyday utilitarian items can fulfill a unique and decorative purpose.

ARCH the ceiling of an elongated walkway to add an interesting architectural detail.

COLLECT kitchen heirlooms passed down through the generations. A cherished rolling pin; a vintage butcher block; a set of cast-iron pans;

or a classic mixer make for conversation-starting decor imbued with sentimental value.

CONSIDER a glass-front refrigerator to create a sense of openness in a small kitchen, if you aren't afraid to display its contents.

MIX and match cabinet hardware in a variety of styles and finishes

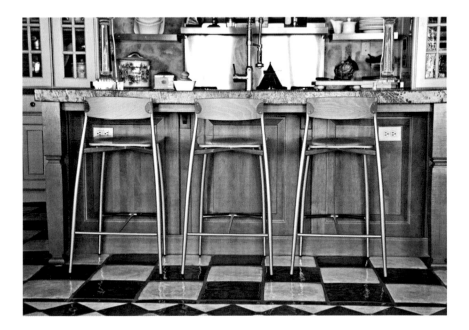

{ GARNISH }

Creative Suggestions

Request handwritten recipes from friends and family that can be framed for display and eventually passed on to future generations.

Hang pot holders on ornamental wall hooks. When used as accessories, they make a colorful statement. Make sure they're within easy reach of the stove.

Brighten dark corners and add some extra glow by placing miniature table lamps throughout a kitchen.

> **TONYA TIP:** Start a handwritten recipe exchange with family members. Commit to trading favorite recipes at least once every year either during Thanksgiving or Christmas. Over the years, you'll have a nostalgic collection of personalized family memories.

HOMEOWNER &
DESIGNER:
Tonya Olsen

White Done Right

The **kitchen renovation** of a **1960s ranch-style home** transformed from outdated Americana to **modern industrial**. Shades of **warm white** and **natural wood** keep the space **open** and **airy**.

PALETTE

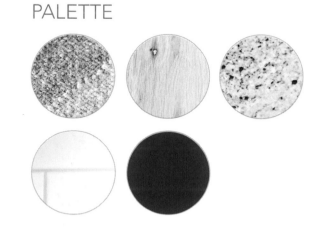

{ INGREDIENTS }

1 APRON SINK

The clean profile of this stainless steel apron front sink is a modern take on a farmhouse classic.

2 BARSTOOLS

Rustic industrial barstools add character while complementing the straight lines and mass of the island.

3 PANTRY

An awkward corner was converted into a walk-in pantry.

4 OPEN SHELVING

White dishes and clear glasses are casually stacked on open shelves. Emerald-green bottles provide a pop of color from the top shelf.

5 FLOORING

White oak flooring adds a farmhouse feel. A light whitewash finish tones down the golden hues while letting the warmth shine through.

6 LIGHTING

A linear brushed-steel frame holds glass panels to create a minimalistic yet distinct light fixture. Vintage filament bulbs cast an ambient glow.

7 HARDWARE

Contemporary brushed nickel pulls are paired with antique glass knobs, adding an eclectic touch.

ROOM RECIPE

{ TONYA'S TAKE }

My favorite features in this kitchen are the open shelves and walk-in pantry. Accessing everyday dishes we use the most is easy and convenient. The small but efficient walk-in pantry is a must-have for every kitchen.

DEFINE a backsplash from countertop to ceiling to prevent choppiness and to visually expand the height of the space.

INSTALL cabinet handles horizontally to create uniformity and visually expand the width of the space.

WARM up whites with wood floors. White cabinets and stainless steel appliances can feel cold and sterile without the rustic wood floor underfoot.

KEEP countertop storage minimal. Glass canisters with lids store baking provisions like flour and sugar. An oversize glass canister holds healthy snacks.

PAINT or stain the island a dark, complementary color. The warm gray color anchors the light and airy kitchen.

{ GARNISH }

Magnetic Memo Panel

Every kitchen deserves a spot for posting memos, favorite recipes, and grocery lists. If wall space is limited, convert the inside of the most often-used pantry or cabinet door into command central.

Ingredients:

Pantry or cabinet door

21-gauge aluminum metal sheet

Construction adhesive (liquid nails)

1. **Measure** inside dimensions of door panel.

2. **Cut** metal sheet to size.

3. **Apply** a ¼" bead of construction adhesive to contact areas on the back of door panel.

4. **Press** aluminum metal sheet firmly into place.

> **TONYA TIP:** Hang a magnetic dry-erase calendar for keeping track of dates and schedules. Keep a cup of dry-erase markers and an eraser nearby.

SLEEP

127

SUNNY SIDE UP

NIGHT AND DAY

A GRAY AREA

HOMEOWNER:
Kassi Capener

DESIGNER:
Pamela Jensen

Come Sail Away

This **understated nautical-themed boy's bedroom** is first class. **Classic** coastal colors in red, blue, and yellow anchor the space without **going overboard.**

PALETTE

{ INGREDIENTS }

1 WINDOW TREATMENTS

A no-sew, faux window shade adds a finishing touch to the room.

2 COLLECTIONS

Rock and seashell collections, handed down from previous generations, are layered in front of an antique board game and vintage maritime artwork.

3 LIGHTING

An inexpensive drum-shaped lampshade adds character to a common ceiling fan.

4 BEDDING

Even children's bedding can be expensive, so a set of pinstriped flat sheets was sewn together to make matching duvet covers.

5 RUGS

A soft-yellow and muted-gray cotton rug fills the empty space on the floor between the twin beds. The wide linear stripes add subtle graphic appeal.

6 PILLOWS

Vibrant throw pillows, in complementary colors and patterns, accessorize each bed. Squares of fabric were sewn back to back to create these easy-to-sew custom pillow covers.

7 ADDITIONAL STORAGE

With two boys in one room, storage space can be limited. Fill storage containers with less-used items and take advantage of the space under the bed.

8 MIRRORS

Brass embellishments add a nautical touch to the corners of a painted mirror, complementing the brass framed porthole mirrors above each bed.

9 CABINET

A salvaged family heirloom, this antique cabinet is used as an open-shelf bookcase. The interior was painted bright red, adding a zing of color to the room.

ROOM RECIPE

{ TONYA'S TAKE }

Interior designer Pamela Jensen knows the ropes when it comes to keeping a themed bedroom from going adrift. I've seen many overdone rooms awash with tacky, nautical accessories and seafaring paraphernalia. Pam was able to tastefully and playfully evoke life at sea without going overboard.

AVOID overdecorating a themed room with a barrage of clichéd accessories. Rather, establish the concept with color and support it with minimal hints of not-so-obvious décor.

ARRANGE furniture, leaving plenty of open floor space for young children to comfortably play with toys.

CHOOSE a theme that is age appropriate or that can easily evolve as children grow.

FRAME vintage maps and ocean charts in rustic driftwood frames. These timeless works of art can easily incorporate into other rooms and styles down the road.

COMBINE classic furniture and family heirlooms into the decor no matter what the theme is. This will prevent the room from becoming outdated too quickly.

{ GARNISH }

Ribbon Lamp Shade

It's been done many times before, which is why this easy do-it-yourself embellishment is so popular.

Ingredients:

Ribbon in color of choice

Hot glue gun

Lampshade

Scissors

1. Cut ribbon to length.

2. Apply a dot of hot glue to one end of the ribbon and press firmly along the seam of the lampshade.

3. Apply another dot of glue a few inches away, pressing and smoothing ribbon around the bottom edge of the lampshade as you go.

4. Repeat steps until ribbon reaches starting point.

5. Add a final dot of glue to the end, slightly overlapping the starting point.

6. Repeat steps 1–5 along the top edge of the lampshade.

> TONYA TIP: Ruffles, rope, beads, and buttons—the options for jazzing up a lampshade are limitless.

Duvet Cover

A duvet made of flat sheets eliminates a step in the bed-making process in the hopes the boys will actually make their bed.

Ingredients:

2 flat sheets sized to fit bed

Sewing machine

Thread

Pins

Buttons

Tape measure

Comforter insert

1. Align sheets face-to-face, securing in place along three sides with pins.

2. Sew three sides of sheets together, leaving one of the short ends open. Measure and mark the location of the buttonholes.

3. Use the buttonhole feature on the sewing machine to add buttonholes on one side of the open end.

4. Sew buttons on the other side of the open end, making sure they line up with the holes.

5. Turn the duvet right side out and insert the comforter.

6. Button holes and make bed!

> TONYA TIP: Use a different pattern on each side of the duvet. Add a coordinating ruffle or trim.

HOMEOWNER &
DESIGNER:
Deboni Sacre

Assisted by
Heather Lewellyn

Double Impact

A **unique palette** of **rich colors** mixed with **soft pastels** and **vibrant hues** is the basis for this stunning girl's bedroom. A **spare twin bed** provides an additional spot for **overnight guests.**

PALETTE

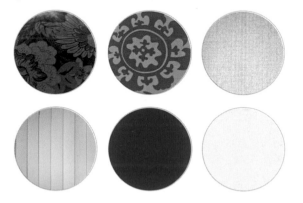

{ INGREDIENTS }

1 BEDS
Custom upholstered headboards pack a visual punch on each bed. Soft curves define the high arch and add a feminine touch. White bedding keeps the overall look clean and crisp. A colorful lumbar pillow ties everything in the room together.

2 CHAIR
A salvaged antique chair, painted a soft shade of buttercream and reupholstered in fun floral fabric, finds a new home in front of a small vanity.

3 DRESSER
A classic chest of drawers serves double duty as a dresser and nightstand. Painted teal, it complements the mini coral lamps sitting on top.

4 LIGHT
An old chandelier comes to life with a few coats of coral spray paint, making it more modern and less shabby chic.

5 WINDOW TREATMENTS
A bleached burlap valance, lined with teal ribbon, adds texture while the billowy folds in the fabric make it appear soft.

6 CEILING
Tongue-and-groove painted a soft, buttery yellow, nestles between white faux beams in the vaulted ceiling. The contrast between the dark walls and mellow ceiling creates a dramatic architectural impact.

ACCESSORIES
Every little girl deserves an antique sterling silver hand mirror and brush to use at her vanity; accessories are kept to a minimum; a blessing gown stays perfectly preserved for future use behind a framed sheet of glass; an empty frame, hung by a swath of fabric, highlights a single, mounted initial; and a white curtain tacked to a vanity with blue ribbon cleverly conceals unsightly duct work.

ROOM RECIPE

{ TONYA'S TAKE }

The combination of elements in this bedroom is a juxtaposition of softness and strength, youth and sophistication, coziness and expansion. The velvety blue walls, an unexpected color choice for a young girl's bedroom, offset the vaulted ceilings. A large window lets in plenty of natural light. This timeless bedroom will effortlessly transition into young adulthood.

CREATE impact and drama by highlighting architectural details using contrast.

APPLY basic interior design principles when decorating with an unusual palette. Scale, symmetry, repetition, and balance keep this room in check.

SHAKE things up a bit by stepping outside of traditional themes and color palettes. Take a chance with daring color combinations.

STORE toys and games in the closet. They are easily accessible yet remain out of sight when not in use.

Faux Bed Skirt Panels

To create the illusion of a fully upholstered bed frame, order extra fabric from the headboard to make a matching twin-sized bed skirt.

Ingredients:

3–5 yards of fabric, depending on pattern repeat

Safety pins

Sewing machine

Measuring tape

Scissors

1. **Measure** the length and height of the mattress.

2. **Add** 1–2 inches to length for seam allowance.

3. **Add** 5–6 inches to height to allow room for pinning to mattress.

4. **Cut** fabric to measurements. Seam together the fabric.

5. **Iron** and safety pin bed panels to the sides and end of the mattress.

> **TONYA TIP:** For an eclectic twist, use fabric in a pattern or color for the bed skirt that contrasts with the headboard and bedding.

HOMEOWNER &
DESIGNER:
Deboni Sacre

Assisted by
Heather Lewellyn

Room for Renewal

A **mix of old and new furniture** in a

variety of classic styles sets the

traditional style of this **master bedroom.**

PALETTE

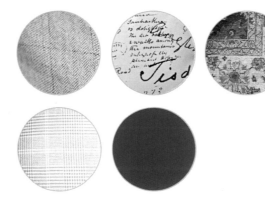

BEFORE

{ INGREDIENTS }

1 RUG

An antique area rug was purposely installed upside down to expose the back, revealing the textural weave and muted colors.

2 PILLOWS

An assortment of throw pillows adorn the expansive bed in a mix of organic textures, traditional patterns, and durable fabrics.

3 CEILING

Paint-grade molding was added to the vaulted ceiling for an inexpensive, yet classy ceiling treatment.

4 BEDSIDE CABINETS

A refurbished console paired with a faux bamboo chair on one side of the bed balances an heirloom, vintage dresser on the other. Although mismatched, these pieces are similar in size and scale. The exaggerated size of the wall clock is balanced by the stacked artwork above the console.

5 WINDOW TREATMENTS

Store-bought curtain panels are layered over a burlap roman shade to create a custom window treatment.

6 LIGHTING

Simple candle sconces cast a subtle glow while reflecting the traditional style.

ACCESSORIES

A trio of ceramic artichokes lines the dresser, adding interest and texture; a sterling silver julep cup holds a petite bouquet of flowers; a pair of wire chicks roost atop a stack of books; and a grouping of mirrors in round rustic frames reflect light above the headboard.

ROOM RECIPE

{ TONYA'S TAKE }

Despite the formal area rug, antique furniture, and traditional style of this space, this master bedroom resonates casual, comfortable livability.

PAINT a wood bed frame a neutral color so it doesn't compete with other finishes in the room.

ESTABLISH a comfortable seating arrangement in front of the windows, providing an additional spot for lounging while enjoying the stream of natural light.

MIX masculine patterns such as houndstooth and tartan with feminine fabrics in soft, neutral colors to create a harmonious balance.

ACCESSORIZE with flowers. Even a small bouquet of fresh flowers makes a statement and will instantly brighten up any space.

PAINT the walls a rich, dark color such as navy, charcoal, or chocolate brown to create a cozy, intimate feeling . . . especially in the master bedroom.

MIX metals. Rust, polished silver, brass, and wrought iron add variety and contrast.

Burlap Faux Roman Shade

This no-sew window treatment is something even a novice can throw together.

Ingredients:

Burlap

1 x 2 MDF board cut to width of window

Staple gun and staples

Needle and thread

Mounting screws

1. **Cut** burlap to the width and length of window.

2. **Staple** top edge of burlap to MDF board, making sure the rough edge is on the backside.

3. **Create** folds in bottom of shade by loosely rolling them to desired length.

4. **Use** the needle and thread to stitch folds in place.

5. **Mount** MDF board to ceiling or wall with screws.

> **TONYA TIP:** Burlap is an inexpensive, organic fabric. The rough texture of burlap complements a variety of styles. It is available in a variety of neutral shades and different textures.

HOMEOWNER:
Kathleen Hermann

DESIGNER:
Rick Boyles

Bohemian Rhapsody

A whitewashed foundation serves

as a clean canvas in this master bedroom

full of vintage treasures.

PALETTE

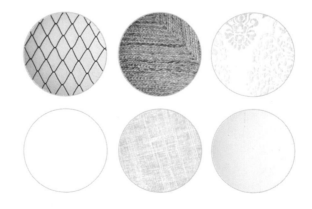

{ INGREDIENTS }

1 BED
Carved detailing and soft, sweeping curves highlight the antique bed frame. Large-scale, floor-length mirrors fill the empty corner behind the headboard, adding an expansive feeling to the space.

2 MANNEQUINS
Vintage dress forms are draped with handmade jewelry. Timeworn, tattered fabric adds a touch of character.

3 DRESSER
An early twentieth-century dresser gets a second life with a coat of peacock-blue paint. The original hardware maintains the authenticity.

4 ARTWORK
An original oil painting by Sherry Dooley leaning atop a rustic cabinet serves as a focal point. The artwork is central to a whimsical vignette of interesting objects.

5 GATE
The salvaged gate of a rusty chain-link fence makes a unique and simple wall decoration.

6 WINDOW TREATMENTS
Velvet damask curtains were installed inside out to reveal the reverse pattern in opposite colors.

7 VANITY
A salvaged desk was converted into a dressing table and discreetly tucked away into a closet nook. A cabinet hutch with glass doors provides open storage for personal items.

8 FLOORING
Recycled hardwood floors, painted a glossy white, reflect the light and serenity of the room. A formerly discarded natural-fiber area rug adds a layer of warmth and texture under the bed.

ROOM RECIPE

{ TONYA'S TAKE }

Less is more in this light and airy master bedroom. An unexpected oasis, the room's soothing palette and minimal decor are a distinct departure from the bold colors in the rest of the house. An uncomplicated collection of treasures keeps the room open and bright.

COLLECT hand-me-downs, salvaged items, and family heirlooms. Afraid to design an entire space with flea market finds? Add a sense of nostalgia by subtly incorporating individual items into existing décor.

INTRODUCE a softer version of the home's eclectic style in a separate room. Because of the neutral palette, it may appear this room is out of place with the rest of the home, but the bohemian elements speak loud and clear.

ANGLE a bed in the corner. The diagonal placement, directly across from the door draws guests into the room while creating a visual focal point.

ACCENT a neutral space with one item in a bold contrasting color. The eye-catching vintage dresser, painted a vivid blue, reflects coordinating pops of color throughout the room.

EMBRACE rusty iron, chipped glass, peeling paint, and weathered wood. Aged imperfections add character to any space.

{ GARNISH }

Creative Suggestion:

Estate, yard, and garage sales are in full force once the weather warms up. Check local classified for times, dates, and locations. Make a girls trip out of it and spend an afternoon hunting for treasures with friends.

HOMEOWNER &
DESIGNER:
Robert McArthur

Sunny Side Up

The **neutral palette** of this **master bedroom**

creates a **perfect foundation** for the

luxurious gold accent wall behind the bed.

PALETTE

BEFORE

{ INGREDIENTS }

1 BED

The simple composition of this custom-designed, one-of-a-kind four-poster bed creates a minimalist aesthetic.

2 CHAIRS

Luxurious yet understated, classic Donghia occasional chairs complement and enhance the space while providing additional seating.

3 CEILING

Whitewashed wood planks on the vaulted ceiling contribute to the modern, rustic appeal of this room. A contemporary dual-blade ceiling fan adds interest and function.

4 FIREPLACE

The ornately detailed plaster relief on fireplace surround is painted white to avoid competing with the eclectic steel mantel and tiled hearth.

5 DRESSER

The sophisticated and elegant dresser adds a vintage touch.

6 READING NOOK

A built-in reading nook with plenty of shelves and storage is cleverly carved out of an unused corner. A shuttered opening overlooks the adjacent stairway and loft.

7 LAMPS

From the permanent collection of the Museum of Modern Art, classic Tizio table lamps add contemporary contrast and an industrial touch.

8 DECORATIVE DETAILS

A crystal doorknob creatively paired with a contemporary house number introduces the diverse design style of the room.

ACCESSORIES

Americana throw pillows add interest to the bed while vintage linen throw pillows fill the nook; an assorted collection of storage containers occupy the nightstands; and a beautiful oil painting in an elegant gold frame is the pièce de résistance.

ROOM RECIPE

{ TONYA'S TAKE }

The brilliance of this room is the gold accent wall. The rest of the room and its contents are all neutral, cream, gray, black, and white. The ornate frame on the oil painting above the fireplace cleverly creates visual balance.

PAINT one wall a vibrant color while keeping the rest of the room neutral.

TOSS in a few unexpected accessories. Notice the American flag pillow on the bed. Its small size adds a whimsical flair without being overwhelming.

MIX cottage with contemporary, and rustic with modern. The white walls and neutral carpet provide a clean palette for multiple styles to work together.

INSTALL a wall treatment to a vaulted ceiling. Whitewashed, rough-hewn planks in various lengths and widths add a rustic architectural detail.

SPRINKLE with simple, decorative do-it-yourself projects to add a personal sense of accomplishment.

Wooden Wall Peg Rack

A practical and easy solution for creating a wall peg rack. Painted the same color as the accent wall, it subtly blends into the design and function of the room.

Ingredients:

Wooden dowel ½″–1″ thick

1 x 3 paint-grade trim board

Drill and wood boring drill bit the same size as dowel

Wood glue

Hammer

1. Determine the length of your board. Cut trim board to appropriate length.

2. Divide the length of the board equally into the number of pegs desired. Make a mark for each peg.

3. Cut dowel into 3″–4″ pieces, angling one of the ends of each piece.

4. Bore appropriate number of holes into the wood.

5. Apply glue to angled end of dowel and insert one peg into each hole. Tap lightly with hammer to secure.

Night and Day

What's **black** and **white** and **Zen** all over?

A **striking master bedroom** uses **black**,

white, and **natural elements** to

create a **restful retreat**.

PALETTE

{ INGREDIENTS }

1 HEADBOARD

An oversize tufted headboard creates a focal point. The height of the headboard matches the height of the windows on either side, creating the illusion of a much larger wall behind the bed.

2 BEDDING

Textures, patterns, and subtle shades in a neutral color palette keep the bed simple yet sophisticated.

3 DRESSER

The clean lines and timeless beauty of a mid-century modern dresser are the perfect style for the space.

4 SEATING

A cozy club chair provides a comfortable seat for reading or putting on shoes.

5 WINDOW TREATMENTS

Clean-lined window panels in soft gray linen frame the windows and impart a sophisticated backdrop behind the bed.

6 PILLOWS

Layered throw pillows in a variety of patterns, shapes, and sizes add a subtle hint of texture to the king-size bed.

7 RUG

A faux fur area rug anchors a sleek black leather bench while offering texture and warmth to the room.

8 LIGHTING

A drum shade within a drum shade adds interest to an otherwise mundane ceiling fixture.

ACCESSORIES

Playful bookends keep a set of books for nighttime reading corralled on the nightstand; sharp radial lines emanate from a small circular mirror; an assortment of simple accessories, including a live plant, create a vignette on the dresser; and a small ivory side table with modern, distressed wooden legs fills the space next to the club chair.

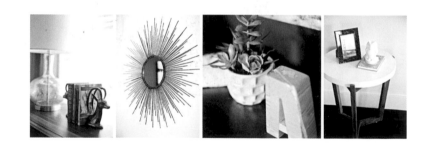

ROOM RECIPE

{ TONYA'S TAKE }

Serenity. Balance. Nature. Principle tenets of Zen style and Asian-influenced decor. This modern sanctuary feels like the ultimate respite for peace, inspiration, and a good night's sleep. Om.

CREATE balance by arranging furniture symmetrically. The bed is anchored by matching nightstands and lamps.

ADD warmth with natural elements. The subtle grain and rich, golden hue make the mid-century modern dresser glow against dark-stained wood floors. Driftwood wall décor also adds texture.

PAINT a room black to create a feeling of expansion. Black walls bookend the room and visually create an illusion of endless space.

HANG window panels on interior French doors, which can be pulled closed for privacy.

{ GARNISH }

Black-and-White Canvas Art

Make a personal statement with an oversize canvas of your favorite black-and-white photograph. Many retailers such as Wal-Mart or Costco have online photo centers that will transform your memories into works of art. Simply upload your high-resolution images, choose the size that will work the best, and voilà, it's as simple as that. Large oversize images or a collection of smaller images can make a huge impact in practically any space.

HOMEOWNER &
DESIGNER:
Emily Carter

Assisted by
Deboni Sacre

A Gray Area

Playful **pops** of **yellow** accentuate

a **neutral gray foundation** in

this **adorable nursery.**

PALETTE

{ INGREDIENTS }

1 CRIB
A classic black crib is a simple furniture choice for the space.

2 CHAIRS
Traditional leather club chairs flank the bay window. They add a masculine, grown-up addition to the room, but a colorful throw pillow softens the look.

3 ARTWORK
Animal art, painted on weathered wood panels, is a modern DIY addition to the nursery.

4 MOBILE
A pinwheel mobile in bright colors and patterns dangles from the ceiling, a few feet from the crib.

5 WINDOW TREATMENTS
Bold horizontal stripes were painted on a canvas drop cloth to create an inexpensive window treatment. Each panel was stapled to the wall in between the false pleats. A string of fabric pennants pulls them together.

6 RUG
A zebra rug adds interest to the open floor space and ties in with the animal motif.

7 DRESSER
Black-and-white strips of checked fabric were spray-mounted to the drawer fronts of an old dresser.

8 WALL TREATMENT
A large metallic grid was painted on the feature wall behind the crib.

ACCESSORIES
Twigs wrapped in bright yellow yarn and placed in a mason jar add height, color, and interest; a brightly painted ornate picture frame serves as a tray for displaying personal items; and mismatched letters playfully spell "OWEN" above the crib.

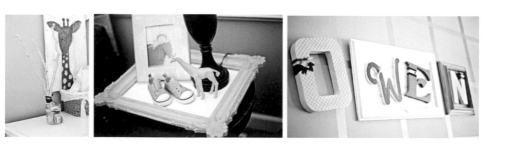

ROOM RECIPE

{ TONYA'S TAKE }

This is a perfect example of how a creative homeowner, with the assistance of professional interior designer Deboni Sacre of LIV Showroom, can create a one-of-a-kind nursery.

USE different shades and sheens of the same paint color to create contrast.

REPEAT colors in a variety of patterns such as animal prints, horizontal stripes, grids, and checks. Variations of black and white pull the room together.

ADD texture with a natural-fiber area rug. The rug subtly frames the contrasting animal print rug on top of it.

Zebra Rug

Animal print rugs are always a fun addition to any room. The creamy background softens the contrasting dark stripes without diminishing the overall impact.

Ingredients:

2 quarts of latex paint in contrasting colors

Canvas drop cloth

Iron

Scissors

Pencil

Polyurethane

1. Iron the drop cloth, smoothing out any creases or folds.

2. Spread the drop cloth on the floor in an open area.

3. Fold it in half, aligning each end.

4. Draw half of an animal shape, starting and ending on the fold.

5. Cut along pencil line.

6. Lay flat.

7. Paint the base color. Let dry.

8. Carefully sketch a symmetrical pattern of stripes on the canvas.

9. With the contrasting color, carefully fill in the pattern. Let dry.

10. For protection, add a coat of polyurethane.

> **TONYA TIP:** If free-handing animal stripes makes you nervous, check the Internet for simple patterns to use as a guide.

Canvas Curtain Panels

Transform a painter's drop cloth into floor-to-ceiling curtain panels. Hang them au naturel or paint a bold design. Either way, these inexpensive window treatments will make a statement.

Ingredients:

Canvas drop cloth, sized to length

Quart latex paint

Painter's tape

Staple sun and staples

Curtain rod

Clip-on curtain rings

1. Canvas drop cloths come hemmed along each edge, so if the size is right, there's no need to adjust.

2. Use a quart of latex paint and a roll of painter's tape to create a geometric pattern.

3. Staple the panel directly to the wall, in between the folds.

4. Hang the panel from a rod using clip-on curtain rings.

5. Tint panels the perfect shade using fabric dye.

> **TONYA TIP:** Add banding, ribbon, buttons, and more. The possibilities are endless!

WORK

173

HOMEOWNER:
Kassie Capener

DESIGNER:
Pamela Jensen

Den Revival

den (*n.*) a **room**, **often secluded**, in a **house** or **apartment**, designed to provide a **quiet**, **comfortable**, and **informal atmosphere** for conversation, reading, writing, and **so on**.

PALETTE

BEFORE

{ INGREDIENTS }

1 STORAGE CABINET

A refurbished dresser comes to life with poppy-red paint and updated hardware. The vivid color explodes against the dark wood paneling.

2 PILLOW

The flavorful Ikat pattern in these accent pillows brings a tribal feel to the space.

3 WINDOW TREATMENTS

Subtle red ticking stripes set against textured linen add height and softness to the space in these custom-made curtain panels.

4 RUG

A large chocolate-brown area rug with a graphic pattern anchors the room.

5 CORK

Installing cork on the back of the bookshelf breaks up the dark wood and hides cords.

ACCESSORIES

The original built-in bookcase displays an assortment of books and personal collections; zesty colors in a bullfight painting add international flair; the bright fuchsia lettering in this pair of authentic posters loudly announce a Spanish bullfight; and vertical stacks of books make a simple table arrangement.

ROOM RECIPE

{ TONYA'S TAKE }

The groovy 1970s paneling brings to mind a sense of nostalgia in this retro den. Subdued lighting and vivid colors make it the coziest room in the house.

KEEP original architectural features, such as the wood paneling, and update it with modern elements such a sunny colors, personal mementos, and a collection of artwork.

STACK books on shelves, tables, and cabinets as an accessory to add a sculptural feel. Place a colorful vase or interesting artifact on top.

HANG framed prints and artwork in front of a bookcase, creating a layered effect and adding depth and dimension.

ADD comfortable guest seating. Warm leather club chairs are a classic addition to this den.

ACCENT a dark space with lamps, sconces, and recessed lighting. Task lighting softly illuminates the surrounding area while preventing eyestrain that can develop from harsh light.

{ GARNISH }

Painted Office Dresser

Repurpose an old dresser with a coat of paint and new hardware. Used in the office, the drawers of a dresser provide additional storage.

Ingredients:

Dresser

Primer

Paint in color of choice

Polyurethane

Fine-grit sand paper

Foam paint roller

Paintbrush

Hardware

1. **Remove** existing hardware.

2. **Clean** dresser thoroughly with a damp cloth.

3. **Sand** the dresser lightly, moving in the direction of the wood grain.

4. **Wipe** off residue with damp cloth.

5. **Add** a coat of primer. Let dry.

6. **Repeat** steps 3–5.

7. **Roll** on 2–3 light coats of paint with foam roller letting each coat dry in between.

8. **Seal** with a final coat of polyurethane.

9. **Install** new hardware.

> **TONYA TIP:** Cover the drawer fronts with a bold pattern, using wallpaper, fabric, or paint.

Working Class

An **assortment of framed art**, a **collection of antique furniture**, and a **sparking crystal chandelier**, all previously tucked away in a basement bedroom, **transform** this otherwise neutral room into a **glamorous study**.

PALETTE

{ INGREDIENTS }

1 | SOFA
Sink into this stylish sofa with the morning paper or a good book. A rich tone-on-tone damask adds luxe appeal.

2 | HUTCH
A vibrant green paint skimmed with a metallic sheen reinvented this hutch into a timeless statement piece.

3 | SECRETARY DESK
A family heirloom, this writing desk is the perfect spot to revive the art of the handwritten letter.

4 | RUG
The rich colors in this precious needlepoint area rug create a formal, sophisticated focal point while drawing the eye down from the high ceiling.

5 | ARTWORK
An asymmetrical gallery wall full of original art, including two authentic Renoir sketches, makes a strong artistic and visual statement while providing inspiration.

6 | LIGHTING
A vintage chandelier exudes timeless elegance with a hint of shimmering opulence.

ACCESSORIES
A greeting card rack displays cards and stationary, conveniently located next to the writing desk; a stack of books becomes a simple pedestal for displaying objects; a set of miniature magnifying glasses double in function and décor; and seashells and sand, collected from a family vacation, fill a pretty ceramic bowl.

ROOM RECIPE

{ TONYA'S TAKE }

A little bit of time spent "home shopping" turned up a goldmine of heirloom furniture, original artwork, and an antique rug—just to name a few. With the assistance and objective perspective of designer Jenna Rix, Kristen saw her old items in a brand-new light!

USE what you have. With an open mind, peruse your home and consider new possibilities. Envision existing items in a new color or with updated hardware. Your home is full of hidden treasures just waiting to be displayed.

CREATE a space that reflects your sense of style. The refined atmosphere of this regal workspace adorned with expensive art, timeless antiquities, and sumptuous textiles, whole heartedly resonates with the homeowner.

ADD a lively palette of pillows in various fabrics, shapes, and patterns to a workspace. The bright colors introduce a playful touch and soften the space while providing a layer of comfort. Pillows can easily be tossed aside to make sitting room for guests.

FORGO window treatments to allow an abundance of natural light. Studies show that natural light in a home office can increase productivity, reduce fatigue, and improve mood.

{ GARNISH }

Terrarium

A quick, easy, and inexpensive homemade terrarium adds a touch of serenity and a little bit of life to the office.

Ingredients:

Glass container of choice, preferably with wide mouth for easy access

Variety of low-maintenance plants such as mini ferns, succulents, and air plants.

Live moss such as reindeer moss

Two parts potting mix, one part sand

Charcoal

Mesh

Pebbles

1. Place pebbles into bottom of glass container for drainage.

2. Cut mesh to fit snugly over the pebbles, making sure the soil and pebbles don't mix.

3. Add a thin layer of charcoal to lightly cover mesh.

4. Add 1 to 2 inches of soil and sand mixture to ensure proper drainage.

5. Add moss and plants, landscaping in an asymmetrical, balanced design.

6. Use a spray bottle to water plants every few days.

> **TONYA TIP:** Clear or transparent containers work the best. Tinted or frosted containers obstruct light, and can impede the growth of the plants.

Ebony and Ivory

Ebony and ivory live together

in **perfect harmony** in this **dramatic,**

color-blocked craft room.

PALETTE

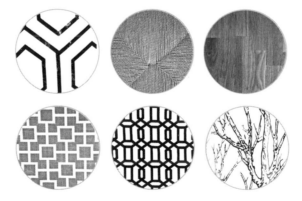

{ INGREDIENTS }

1 LIGHT
Hang an oversize decorative pendant in the center of a small room while providing task lighting in a work area.

2 DESK
A desk with wide drawers provides storage for large sheets of paper and artwork. Remove some of the drawers and replace with a basket that can easily be toted around the room.

3 FLOORING
Durable flooring in a work area is easier to maintain if spills happen. The distressed finish will disguise future mishaps.

4 STORAGE
Provide plenty of storage in multiple locations throughout a craft room.

5 CORKBOARD
A wall mounted corkboard is a practical element in a craft area.

ROOM RECIPE

{ TONYA'S TAKE }

You would never know this cleverly disguised craft room is actually a basement storage room. Black and white vibrates in stark contrast to get the creative juices flowing!

PAINT concrete floors with an exterior floor paint in a craft room. The durable finish is resistant to potential spills and messes.

PROVIDE multiple workstations for various tasks. A sewing table, a desk, and a counter-height table provide three zones for separate activities. Each table is a different height to comfortably accommodate projects that require either standing or sitting.

KEEP accessories to a minimum. Busy, colorful decor can sometimes be distracting.

HANG window panels above and beyond the window frame to visually enlarge the space. White window panels hung against white walls prevent the eye from being drawn to the window well.

Twine Pendant

This homemade, oversize pendant makes a crafty statement while illuminating a warm glow.

Ingredients:

Inflatable exercise ball approximately 55 cm

Twine

Clear wallpaper paste

Electrical cord socket

Scissors

Lightbulb

1. Cover twine in wallpaper paste while wrapping around exercise ball.

2. Wrap twine several times around and in overlapping directions.

3. Let dry for several days.

4. With a sharp object, pop the exercise ball and let it slowly deflate.

5. Cut exercise ball into pieces and carefully remove between twine.

6. Cut a small opening at the top of the finished pendant.

7. Install lightbulb into socket and insert cord into opening.

8. Hang pendant from ceiling.

TONYA TIP: Use colorful yarn in place of twine to cast a chromatic hue.

TONYA TIP: Create your own template out of cardboard or purchase an existing one online or at a local craft store.

Painted Floor

A painted floor is an inexpensive way to cover less than-perfect concrete. The bold geometric pattern adds drama to the space.

Ingredients:

Alkaline degreaser

Exterior concrete floor paint in colors of choice

Template

Painter's tape

Paintbrush and paint roller

Polyurethane

1. Thoroughly clean the concrete with alkaline degreaser and allow floor to dry.

2. Paint floor with darkest paint color and allow it to dry for two days.

3. Position template to floor and adhere with painter's tape.

4. Apply lightest paint color to open areas of the floor. Let dry.

5. Reposition template and continue steps 3–4 until room is complete. Let dry for 48 hours.

6. Seal entire area with polyurethane and let dry several days before allowing foot traffic.

Fun Follows Function

This **family workspace** is the **creative hub** of the home. **Abstract** yet **organized,** the **effervescent color palette** inspires a **playful approach** to **work.**

PALETTE

{ INGREDIENTS }

1 CLOSET

Shut the door on messy-looking, unorganized memo boards. Corkboard, covered in colorful fabric, is encased in the closet panels.

2 SEATING

Guests have a place to relax in these classic club chairs, embellished with fabric banding and oversize nail heads.

3 WORK CABINET

This sensible storage cabinet stores supplies in style. A stagecoach shade conceals the printer and other unsightly items.

4 STORAGE

Casters add functional style to a low-profile bookcase, which tucks neatly under the window.

5 WINDOW TREATMENTS

Café-style shutters cover the lower portion of the window, letting an ample amount of natural light. Bamboo roller shades can easily retract to offer privacy.

6 INSPIRATION BOARD

A framed and upholstered bulletin boards is a practical but decorative detail.

7 RUGS

Layered rugs add dimension, texture, color, and pattern, cohesively tying the furniture together.

ACCESSORIES

A glass canister corrals stray tape measures, a tool of the trade for interior designers; ceramic birds take flight around the bulletin board establishing a bird theme; a vignette of office accessories is pretty and practical next to a lovely task lamp; a collection of globes adds color and interest; a vintage telephone (that really works!) adds a touch of nostalgia and assures that the phone is always in the same spot; a rustic bird house visually echoes the bird theme; and the bird profile on this retro modern cuckoo clock is repetitious of the bird motif while the clock itself mirrors the other wall clocks.

ROOM RECIPE

{ TONYA'S TAKE }

This is the most-used room in our house, and for good reason. The playful colors and lighthearted décor encourage family members to gravitate to this space. One end of the room is open to a small family room making it conveniently located and accessible.

KEEP unsightly clutter tucked away and out of sight. The printer, reams of paper, and other office necessities are stored in a media cabinet. Using colorful thumbtacks and a swatch of fabric, a functional stagecoach shade was attached to the front concealing equipment and supplies. Likewise, a narrow closet houses notebooks, binders, and miscellaneous items.

PROVIDE a stash of snacks for munching on during those long work hours. Display clear glass canisters with nuts, candy, or other goodies.

USE an accent chair for desk seating. Don't limit yourself to a black utilitarian office chair on wheels.

FILL an office space with inspirational and motivational reminders. A large wooden sign spells out family rules while metal letters spell out "BE" on the bookshelf.

Upholstered Corkboard Panels

Take advantage of the inside of a cabinet or closet door. These clever bulletin boards can be custom sized to fit within any door panels.

Ingredients:

12 x 12 cork wall tiles at least ¼" thick

Quilt batting

Fabric of choice, cut to size

Cardboard

Duct tape

Utility knife

Metal ruler

Permanent marker

Staple gun and staples

1. **Determine** the size of the door panels by measuring the length and width.

2. **Draw** a template approximately ⅛" smaller than the door panel size on the cardboard and carefully cut it out. Arrange cork tiles face down and edge to edge on a large, flat surface if door panels are larger than 12 x 12.

3. **Duct** tape the tiles together along each edge.

4. **Place** cardboard template on the back of the cork tiles and outline the shape with a permanent marker.

5. **Use** the metal ruler and utility knife to cut the shape of the door panel out of the cork tiles.

6. **Duct-tape** the cardboard template to the back of the cork tiles creating a solid back.

7. **Wrap** the corkboard cutout in batting. Tightly secure in place with staples.

8. **Wrap** the corkboard in fabric of choice. Tightly secure in place with staples.

9. **Secure** finished corkboard into door panels.

> **TONYA TIP:** If the corkboards won't fit within the door panel, hang them instead with a pretty ribbon.

Ribbon and Nail Head Chair Embellishment

Adorn furniture with a band of ribbon and decorative nail heads.

Ingredients:

Ribbon of choice

Decorative upholstery nails

Tape measure

Rubber mallet

1. **Lay** chair on its side for easy access.

2. **Measure** the length of each edge of the furniture and determine the spacing for each nail heads.

3. **Starting** in the corner along the bottom edge, tap nail head into ribbon with rubber mallet.

4. **Continue** tapping nail heads into ribbon while pulling ribbon taut around the entire chair.

> **TONYA TIP:** Add ribbon and nail heads to sofas and ottomans or even to a bookshelf or table!

WASH

201

NEW TRADITIONS
228

HOMEOWNER &
DESIGNER:
Robert McArthur

Looking Up

Streaming with natural light, this hardworking laundry room is a versatile as the whimsical elements that adorn it. Beyond washing clothes, this multipurpose room functions as a butler's pantry, mudroom, and potting room.

PALETTE

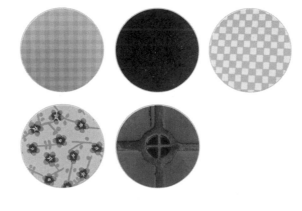

BEFORE

{ INGREDIENTS }

1 SINK

A vintage, wall mount farmhouse sink nestles at the base of a staggered garden window. A soleil medallion radiates amongst the creamy crackled tiles.

2 WASHER DRYER

A custom-built pedestal elevates the washer and dryer to a comfortable height with open storage below for laundry baskets.

3 COUNTERTOPS

Check out the silk-screened laminate countertop. Concrete countertops flank the tile surrounding the farmhouse sink.

4 WALL TREATMENT

Intricately carved wood frame molding replaces the typical chair rail, adding dimension and detail.

5 LAUNDRY BASKET

Sturdy and utilitarian, a commercial laundry cart adds chic-industrial flair.

6 CEILING

Wallpaper on the ceiling? Yep. It draws the eye up and creates an illusion of height.

7 ACCENT TILES

Small accents of custom screen-printed decorative tile make a big impact in this whimsical laundry room.

8 FLOORING

Quartered metallic accent tiles dot the floor between durable yet inexpensive terra-cotta tiles.

ACCESSORIES

Open shelving provides easy access to gardening books and supplies; charming curiosities appear throughout the room; a decorative light switch makes a bright impact; and fanciful desk accessories are near at hand.

ROOM RECIPE

{ TONYA'S TAKE }

Prior to a major renovation, this room served as the kitchen. Centrally located, it's designed as a walk through for access from the new kitchen to the dining room, serving as a butler's pantry. It's also close to the back-door entrance, convenient for using as a potting room.

MAKE it fun. Doing laundry and other chores become more enjoyable when surrounded by creative décor.

COMBINE multiple finishes and styles in coordinating colors and patterns to create balance. Laminate, stone, and tile countertops harmonize surprisingly well with floral wallpaper, terracotta floor tiles, and quaint accessories. Each element contains a small remnant of another element in the room.

INSTALL a pair of narrow double doors in the place of a single door. This architectural detail adds a subtle sense of grandeur.

PLAN ahead. Whether you are starting from scratch or renovating an existing space, plan for an efficient layout centered on task-based design. Include multiple work zones that keep functions separate. Install space saving convenience features like a laundry chute and a built-in ironing board.

INCORPORATE a small TV or computer to provide entertainment while doing mundane chores such as folding laundry.

{ GARNISH }

Creative Suggestions

Even if you can't dedicate an entire room for laundry, a closet can offer a compact solution. Stackable washer and dryers are a good choice in a narrow closet. For example, install a wall-mounted, flat-folding drying rack on the inside panel of the door. If the closet is tall enough and the washer and dryer are compact, install a pedestal below the stackable washer and dryer for storing laundry detergent and other items.

HOMEOWNER &
DESIGNER:
Kristen Holm

Bright Breezeway

A **simple** and **vibrant mudroom**

makes for a **cheerful transition** from

the **outdoor** to the **indoor**.

PALETTE

{ INGREDIENTS }

1   STORAGE

An inexpensive modular bookshelf was converted into a seated bench. The open bins provide storage for shoes with plenty of seating space along the top.

2   WASHTUB CORNER

A handheld shower is a useful feature for washing dogs and muddy boots.

3   HARDWARE

Faux crystals adorn the hooks and doorknobs, adding a gleaming touch of glamour. Glass tiles frame the faucet.

4   DISPLAY

Mudrooms are the perfect place to display family messages. A chicken wire frame and magnetic memo board keep family members up to date as they come and go.

ACCESSORIES

Wall décor is kept to a minimum so as to not overwhelm the small space. Rather, a bright series of canvas prints immediately greet family members as they enter the main part of the house.

ROOM RECIPE

{ TONYA'S TAKE }

The mudroom is otherwise referred to as command central for this busy family. It is the first room family members enter from the garage when they arrive home and the last room they walk through as they leave. It's a perfect transition zone for all the comings and goings.

PROVIDE plenty of large, tightly secured wall hooks for hanging outerwear and heavier equipment like backpacks and sporting equipment. Install heavy-duty hooks into a sheet of wood before mounting on to the wall, reinforce into a stud wall, or anchor into the sheetrock.

IMPLEMENT freestanding furniture and cabinets if built-ins are out of the budget.

INSTALL a miniature shower or utility sink if possible. The mudroom is the most convenient place to rinse garden tools, wash small animals, and clean muddy shoes before entering

the house. A hose connected to the faucet adds another level of functionality.

CHOOSE durable and easy-to-clean mats and rugs. An outdoor floor mat allows guests to wipe their feet before entering the mudroom, while a cotton throw rug leads guests into the house. Both are easy to rinse off or throw in the wash if necessary.

ADD utility baskets for collecting random items. A large wicker basket conveniently collects odds-and-ends and can be carried from room to room when putting things away.

Chicken Wire Frame

This easy to make memo board is a decorative and functional accessory.

Ingredients:

Frame

Chicken wire

Wire cutters

Heavy-duty staple gun and staples

1. **Lay** empty frame facedown on a large, flat surface.

2. **Staple** chicken wire to the back of the frame.

3. **Snip** excess chicken wire around the frame using wire cutters.

4. **Hang** and enjoy!

> **TONYA TIP:** Paint the frame a vibrant color before installing the chicken wire. Use clothespins or bulldog clips to adhere items to the wire. Install in a convenient location such as in a mudroom or a busy doorway.

HOMEOWNER &
DESIGNER:
Jennifer Hudgins

photography by
Amy Herndon

Natural Selection

Rich, **earthy hues** and **organic texture** lay the

foundation for this **recently renovated bathroom.**

As an **added bonus**, an awkward jack-and-jill

walk-through was transformed into a **study area.**

PALETTE

BEFORE

{ INGREDIENTS }

1 SINK

The effervescent glass in this vessel bowl sink certainly makes a statement! A brushed nickel waterfall faucet complements the stainless steel base of the sink.

2 SHOWER

Porcelain tile, an easier-to-maintain alternative for the shower, mimics the blue-gray and rust tones of natural slate. Glass and slate listello outlined with brushed nickel trim add visual interest. Tumbled slate mosaics are a smart and slip-resistant choice for the shower floor. Granite matching the vanity countertop finishes off the bench seat and corner shelves. A clear glass door makes the roomy walk-in shower feel even larger.

3 VANITY

The original vanity was renovated to coordinate with the slate tiles. The vanity was stripped, painted, and glazed to create an aged, rustic look. Simple stainless steel hardware adorn the door fronts. The veins in a slab of granite run perpendicular to the wall, representing running water.

4 STUDY AREA

An antique desk and vintage chair replaced an unused vanity, turning this awkward walk-through into a private study zone.

ROOM RECIPE

Older homes often have odd rooms with hidden potential. Converting this awkward vanity into a study area deserves an A+.

ASSESS the potential needs and uses of a space before renovating. Referred to as the schematic phase interior design, it is important to explore different ways to consider the maximum use of a space.

CONSIDER the space beyond the four walls of a room. The wall behind the original tub and shower divided the bathroom from the attic. The wall was removed, and the space was extended, allowing for a large walk-in shower.

MIX rustic with modern. Natural elements such as slate and granite contrast well with sleek hardware and contemporary light fixtures.

CREATE a vacation-type retreat within your own home. Avid skiers, these homeowners often spend their downtime in mountain getaways. This bathroom remodel was inspired by the warm and welcoming finishes seen in many rustic resorts.

ADD depth and drama by layering recessed, vanity, and spot lighting.

{ GARNISH }

Creative Suggestions

Carving out a place for your children to study might be easier than you think. Underutilized space such as the area under your stairs, an empty closet, or an unused bathroom can easily be converted into a homework zone. Ideally, a nook designated for homework should include the following features:

Minimal distractions

Large, smooth writing surface

Task lighting

Bulletin or memo board

Ample storage

Comfortable seating

HOMEOWNER
& DESIGNER:
Kathleen Hermann

Recycled Restroom

A bohemian mix of **salvaged materials,**

antique **collectibles,** and flea market finds

boldly collide in a **one-of-a-kind**

family bathroom.

PALETTE

{ INGREDIENTS }

1 LIGHTING
A homemade mason jar light fixture replaces the traditional vanity light. Exposed conduit adds an industrial touch.

2 FLOORING
A contrasting floral area rug dresses up the original floor tile.

3 CABINETS
The original vanity was repainted and antiqued. The lower counter height make it possible to hold a vessel sink.

4 STORAGE
The doors were removed on the wall cabinet to create open shelving for assorted mementos.

5 SINK
The natural stone vessel sink blends seamlessly with the plethora of vintage finishes in the room.

6 SHOWER
A clear shower curtain exposes the vintage wall tiles while keeping the space open.

7 COUNTERTOPS
Countertops made of salvaged wood, rescued from a burn pile, add texture, color, and character.

ACCESSORIES
A miniature vintage dresser, used for storage, sits on top of the counter; a wooden hatbox keeps toiletries accessible and tidy; a driftwood lamp emits a golden glow; and a rusted metal shelf disguises an unused door while simultaneously storing towels and linens.

ROOM RECIPE

{ TONYA'S TAKE }

My favorite element of this multifaceted bathroom is the salvaged countertops. The battered planks of wood in various shades of chipped paint establish the room's timeworn quality.

ACCESSORIZE with a common theme in space with elaborate details. Most of the embellishments in this bathroom have a water-related theme, which keeps the look cohesive.

INTRODUCE creative storage options when space is limited. In addition to the vanity, the small antique cabinet and the industrial shelving rack are great examples.

CREATE a focal point with a large, bold piece of art. In a room with so much going on, the vivid oil painting on the far end of the bathroom gives the eye a place to rest.

KEEP dull, aged, or brushed finishes on the metal elements in an excessively rustic space. Avoid the polished and refined.

LAYER accessories to create depth. Artwork and mirrors hang behind casual groupings of eclectic elements.

Recycled Wood Countertop

Upcycling, the act of repurposing waste materials or discarded items into a new product, is the latest trend in eco-friendly, do-it-yourself projects. These recycled countertops not only look great, but they're good for the environment too.

Ingredients:

10–15 2 x 6 x 8 boards

Table saw

Woodworking glue

Belt sander

Fine-grit sandpaper

Woodworking clamps

Polyurethane

1. Cut each board into 5-inch widths.

2. Run a bead of glue along the clean edge of each board.

3. Join boards together and secure at each end with a clamp.

4. Let glue dry according to manufacturer's instructions.

5. Continue steps 2–4 until desired countertop length and width is formed.

6. Smooth the surface with a belt sander.

7. Paint or stain countertop if desired. Lightly sand for a distressed look.

8. Apply several coats of polyurethane, lightly sanding between each dried coat.

TONYA TIP: Mix a variety of wood species in their natural finish to create a butcher-block look.

HOMEOWNER &
DESIGNER:
Robert McArthur

New Traditions

A **modern mix** of **classic materials** gives

this master bathroom a **quaint** and

sophisticated feel.

PALETTE

BEFORE

{ INGREDIENTS }

1 SHOWER

Decorative bronze trim adds a touch of class to staggered white field tiles. A single handmade tile accents the niche.

2 TUB

A jetted soaking tub is tucked away in a quaint alcove. The circular window fills the space with natural light.

3 COUNTERTOP

An apron front adds architectural appeal to the honed soapstone countertops. Oil-rubbed bronze fixtures make them feel even more vintage.

4 CABINETS

The vanity feels open and airy poised atop slim furniture legs. An open shelf niche adds convenience. An oversize wall cabinet provides extra storage above the toilet.

5 WALL TREATMENT

Two-tone wallpaper in rustic red hues contrasts the overall neutral elements of the bathroom. Installing striped wallpaper horizontally visually elongates the small water closet. An eclectic mix of artwork hangs haphazardly on the wall.

6 FLOORING

Made from partially recycled content, these mosaic tiles create a textured illusion on the floor. A single hand-painted tile introduces an identical set of twins on the other side of the bathroom. A handmade rug by a local artist adds a personal flair.

ROOM RECIPE

{ TONYA'S TAKE }

This bathroom reminds me of an updated version of a vintage 1920s bathroom. It has a nostalgic quality with a modern flair. The bathroom has a masculine quality yet has surprising little details that add a feminine touch.

ADD additional lighting to a vanity mirror by installing wall-mount track lights along the sides.

STAGGER cabinet depths, allowing for closer access to the mirror.

SUSPEND base cabinets in a small bathroom to visually enlarge the space. Toe-kick lighting creates a dramatic effect and visually expands the space even more.

DRESS up inexpensive white field tile with pops of decorative tile. You might not be able to afford to tile an entire bathroom in a high-end tile, but mingling it thoughout is an affordable and stylish alternative.

INSTALL a dustpan vacuum along the toe kick of your vanity if your home has a central vacuum system. A small inlet suctions dirt and hair effortlessly off the bathroom floor.

Painted Horizontal Stripes

High-end designer wallpaper doesn't come cheap. Single rolls can start at eighty dollars and range up to five hundred dollars or more, not including installation! Painting a tone on tone stripe is an inexpensive alternative.

Ingredients:

Paint in two similar tones

Paintbrush, roller, and tray

Measuring tape

Level

Painter's tape

1. **Paint** the entire wall the lighter of the two colors. Let dry.

2. **Measure** the height of the wall to determine the width of your stripes.

3. **Adhere** painter's tape to the wall in long, unbroken strips to mark the stripes.

4. **Paint** in between the painter's tape with the darker of the two colors.

5. **Let** dry and remove tape.

> **TONYA TIP:** Keep in mind that more contrast between paint colors will create a more dramatic effect.

APPENDIX

Behind the Scenes

Behind the glamour of a well-designed space are a lot of
hard work and mishaps (and chops) that can go into decorating.

Inspiration & Shopping Resources

MAGAZINES

Better Homes and Gardens
Cottage Style
Country Living
Do It Yourself
Domino
Elle Décor
HGTV Magazine
House Beautiful
Martha Stewart Living
Real Simple
Southern Living

DESIGN SITES

BHG.com
Elledecor.com
Flickr.com
HGTV.com
Housebeautiful.com
Houzz.com
Instagram.com
Pinterest.com

DESIGN BLOGS

alittletipsy.com
amandacarolathome.com
ana-white.com
apartmenttherapy.com
athoughtfulplaceblog.com
brynalexandra.blogspot.com
centsationalgirl.com
dainelleoakeyinteriors.blogspot.com
emilyaclark.blogspot.com
fieldstonehilldesign.com
houseofturquoise.com
littlegreennotebook.blogspot.com
mustardseedinteriors.com
mydesigndump.blogspot.com
ohdeedoh.com
organizeanddecorateeverything.com
queenbeeandme.com
remodelista.com
sandandsisal.com
southernhospitalityblog.com
stylebyemilyhenderson.com
sweetcsdesigns.com
tatertotsandjello.com
the36thavenue.com
thehandmadehome.net
thehouseofsmiths.com
theidearoom.net
theinspiredroom.net
thriftydecorchic.blogspot.com
vintagerevivals.com

SHOPPING

Anthropologie
anthropologie.com

Ballard Designs
ballarddesigns.com

Bellacor
bellacor.com

CB2
cb2.com

Crate and Barrel
crateandbarrel.com

Deseret Industries
deseretindustries.lds.org

Down East Outfitters
downeastoutfitters.com

Goodwill Industries
goodwill.org

Hip and Humble
hipandhumble.com

Home Again
homeagainconsignment.squarespace.com

Home Decorator's Collection
homedecorators.com

Home Depot
homedepot.com

IKEA
ikea.com

Jo-Ann Fabric and Craft Stores
joann.com

Joss & Main
jossandmain.com

Lamp's Plus
lampsplus.com

Land of Nod
landofnod.com

Layla Grace
laylagrayce.com

Lighting Universe
lightinguniverse.com

Lowe's
lowes.com

Minted
minted.com

Nuvo Cabinet Paint
nuvocabinetpaint.com

One King's Lane
onekingslanc.com

PB Teen
pbteen.com

Pier 1 Imports
pier1.com

Pottery Barn
potterybarn.com

Pottery Barn Kids
potterybarnkids.com

Recycled Consign and Design
recycledconsignanddesign.com

Restoration Hardware
restorationhardware.com

River City Trading
facebook.com/pages/
River-City-Trading-Post

Rugs USA
rugsusa.com

Savers
savers.com

Serena and Lily
serenaandlily.com

Shades of Light
shadesoflight.com

Target
target.com

Tuesday Morning
tuesdaymorning.com

Urban Outfitters
urbanoutfitters.com

Walls Wallpaper & Design Boutique
wallsdesignshop.com

Wayfair
wayfair.com

West Elm
westelm.com

World Market
worldmarket.com

Z Gallerie
zgallerie.com

Zinc Door
zincdoor.com

Acknowledgments

When I was approached by the publisher to write an interior design book in December 2012, with a turnaround time of three months, I briefly hesitated. Wait. That's not true. To be totally honest, I so did NOT hesitate, not even for one millisecond. Maybe I should have, but I'm so glad I didn't! My first and only thought was "bring it on." During the twelve weeks I worked on the book, including two major holidays (Christmas and New Year's) and two weeklong bouts with the flu, multitudes of people stepped up to assist with making this happen.

Sara, Sara, bo Bara, fee fy fo Fara, Sara! (I've always wanted to say that for some reason.) I know you didn't realize what you were getting yourself into (yeah, me neither) when you naively agreed to loan me your awesomeness and talent. Thanks so much; I couldn't have done it without you. 444!

The biggest thanks go to my business partners and fellow designers at LIV Showroom, Pamela Jensen, Deboni Sacre, and Kristen Holm. It was no accident that we crossed paths, and I can't wait to see where we go from here. Thank you for reigning me in and keeping me focused. Your suggestions and guidance were invaluable. Thank you for volunteering your personal homes and your clients' homes. You all did an amazing job.

Thank you to all the extremely talented designers and bloggers who willingly contributed their expertise, time, and effort on such short notice. I look up to all of you. You and your spaces truly are inspiring! Each time I left a photo shoot from one of the homes you designed, I walked away with a million ideas. Thank you, Rick Boyles, Aly Brooks, Autumn Clemons, Kirsten Krason, Robert McArthur, Kara Paslay, and Jenna Rix. Thanks,

Rick, I hope to meet you some day soon—you rock! Aly, thank you for letting Cheri recommend you for the book. Your home is a DIY dream. Autumn, if I'd known we had a possessed bathroom on our hands, I never would have gotten you involved. Thanks for hanging in there! Kirsten, your blog, talent, and style are truly inspirational to me; thank you. Robert, thank you for being my inspiration from day one; I can't thank you enough. Jenna, you were the first one I thought of for this book. You have an amazing career ahead of you, and I can't wait to see what you create. Kara, thank you for agreeing to be featured in an interior design book for some random person in Utah. I'll see you on TV!

Thank you to all the homeowners for offering your homes and projects for this book. Your personality and style definitely made each room AMAZING. Kassi Capener, Sally Harvey, Kathleen Hermann, Todd and Jennifer Hudgins, Brian and Rachel Jones, Darrin and Brooke Karras, Garth and Natalie Renfrow, Scott and Lauretta Sechrest, Rob and Tricia Swesey, and Anthony and Bershunda Taylor. Kassi, thank you for letting Pam do pretty much whatever the heck she wanted to do in your house. Thank you, Sally and Rachel, for everything. You truly are my soul sisters. Kathleen, it was pure destiny that I came with Jennifer to pick up her vanity; thank you for agreeing to be in my book on the spot. Jennifer, my bestest warrior monkey visionary friend forever (BWMVFF?), as always, thanks for pulling through for me. Brooke, thanks for wandering into LIV and letting Deboni assist you with the design of your beautiful home. Renfrows and Taylors, thank you for agreeing to showcase your amazing homes in an interior design book for some random person from Utah. Lauretta, thank you for letting your *true* colors shine through your home. Tricia (and Rob!), thank you, thank you, thank you . . . hopefully you've recovered because there's lots more to do.

Thank you to Heather Lewellyn, Samantha Zenger, and Sara Wolfley for assisting on many of the projects.

Thank you to photographers Jessica Mauss and Amy Herndon for pinch-hitting. Your work is amazing.

Amber and Shane McMillan. What's the good news? You deserve to know that I am in sincere gratitude for your friendship, commitment, support, and assistance during the co-creation of your amazing home. Thank you for being open to all the possibilities. There are no accidents! From my heart to yours—love and light.

Jodie and Rachael: I cannot express my depth of gratitude for all of your help during the three months of craziness. Thank you for not jumping on the first plane back to the UK! I never would have been able to accomplish this without your willingness to do whatever needed to be done both at home and at LIV. If I ever need a room painted (then repainted, then scraped clean, then repainted *again*), I know whom to call! Wait. I can't make international calls. Nevermind, you're off the hook.

Thank you, Lyle Mortimer and Cedar Fort Publishing for giving me this incredible opportunity. Haley, Angela, Whitney, Rodney, and everyone else involved, you were an absolute pleasure to work with.

To my boys . . . if you can dodge a ball, you can dodge a wrench (yes, I know it's backwards). Thank you for dodging the big, fat wrench I threw into your lives. Spencer, thank you for being my angel. Love, Mom.

Without further ado, thank you to my husband Jeff for . . . well, being Jeff. I'd have to write another book to list all of the ways you love and support me. Thank you. I love you.

Photographers

SARA BOULTER

saraboulterphotography.com

Sara Boulter is a photographer (and amateur home decorator) based in Salt Lake City, Utah. She's just a girl who loves her job. She takes pictures of amazing people and interesting things. When Sara's not photographing drool-worthy homes or beautiful brides, she's fortunate enough to spend time doing what she loves the most . . . hanging out with family and friends, traveling the globe, eating weird food, snuggling her pets, and feeding her Instagram addiction. Sara feels beyond lucky to have been part of *Room Recipes,* and her sincerest desire is that you will find inspiration within its pages.

For my biggest fan, for my sweetest boy, and for you . . .

JESSICA MAUSS

jessicamaussphotography.com

Jessica Mauss is an award-winning fine art and portrait photographer based in the Phoenix, Arizona, area. She brings her fine art background into all of her work to create art that is both personal and memorable. When she's not behind the camera, Jessica can be found trying to keep up with her three children and husband.

AMY HERNDON

amyherndonphotography.com

Amy Herndon is an on-location, natural light photographer for babies, children and families. She offers sessions in Tulsa, Oklahoma, and is also available for travel. Amy strives to capture the beauty of real life: the innocence, the wonder, the giggles, the imperfections, the joy, the love. Your life . . . captured.

sara boulter photography

Contributors

TONYA OLSEN
LIV Showroom
Bountiful, Utah
livshowroom.com
myroomrecipes.com

KRISTEN HOLM, PAMELA JENSEN, & DEBONI SACRE
LIV Showroom
Bountiful, Utah
livshowroom.com

ALY BROOKS
Entirely Eventful
South Jordan, Utah
entirelyeventful.com

ROBERT MCARTHUR
RGM Studios
Bountiful, Utah
robertgmcarthurstudios.com

SARA BOULTER
Sara Boulter Photography
Farmington, Utah
saraboulterphotography.com

RICK BOYLES
River City Trading Post
Jenks, Oklahoma

JENNA RIX
Design Sparrow
Bountiful, Utah
designsparrow.blogspot.com

KARA PASLAY
Kara Paslay Designs
Tulsa, Oklahoma
karapaslaydesigns.com
tildesigndouspart.com

RANDY & KASSI CAPENER
Brigham City, Utah

KATHLEEN HERMANN
Tulsa, Oklahoma

BRIAN AND RACHEL JONES
Mapleton, Utah

SALLY HARVEY
Cottonwood Heights, Utah

SCOTT & LAURETTA SECHREST
Bountiful, Utah

SHANE & AMBER MCMILLAN
Bountiful, Utah

ANTHONY & BERSHUNDA TAYLOR
Tulsa, Oklahoma

ROB & TRICIA SWESEY
Surprise, Arizona

BROOKE & DARRIN KARRAS
Kaysville, Utah

GARTH & NATALIE RENFROW
Tulsa, Oklahoma

JOHN & EMILY CARTER
Stansbury Park, Utah

Paint Color Index

Index

About the Author

Tonya Olsen has always had a passion for designing charming, budget-friendly interiors. She loves to combine traditional interior design principles with personal, do-it-yourself flair.

Tonya shares ownership of LIV Showroom, a full-service interior design firm and retail showroom, and holds a master's degree in interior design. She is also an interior designer for Utah homebuilder Rainey Homes.

Tonya has over twenty years of professional design experience, bargain-shopping fortitude, and do-it-yourself gumption. She spends her spare time gleaning inspiration from interior design books, magazines, blogs, and websites. Tonya and her husband have three boys and live in their recently renovated home in Bountiful, Utah.